From **The Education Trust**

The Transforming School Counseling national initiative, which began in 1995, believes strongly that PK-12 school counselors are linchpins in the process needed to ensure that every student in our country graduates ready for success in both college and careers. Like all educators, school counselors must be held accountable for their contribution to raising student achievement and closing achievement gaps among students of color, low-income students, and their more advantaged peers. The question now asked of us is "How do school counselors contribute to the academic achievement goals of the school?" To answer this question, school counselors must become data-driven.

In 1999–2000, The Education Trust gathered the school counseling leaders and pioneers for the purpose of developing a model for school counselor accountability. Norm Gysbers, Bob Myrick, Curly Johnson, Reese House, Pat Martin, Sue Reynolds, Carolyn Stone, Jim MacGregor, Fred Bemak, Carol Dahir, and others participated in this series of meetings. Their work resulted in several frameworks, of which MEASURE is one. MEASURE helps school counselors take steps to be consumers of data for the purpose of benefiting students. It is a simple, understandable approach that helps quantify the value that school counselors add to the academic success of all students.

School counselors must step up to the plate as accountable educators focused on forever closing our nation's achievement gaps. MEASURE is a tool to help in this work.

Peggy Hines, Ed.D., Director
The Education Trust's National Center for Transforming School Counseling

SCHOOL COUNSELOR ACCOUNTABILITY
A MEASURE of Student Success

THIRD EDITION

Carolyn B. Stone

University of Florida

Carol A. Dahir

New York Institute of Technology

Boston   Columbus   Indianapolis   New York   San Francisco   Upper Saddle River
Amsterdam   Cape Town   Dubai   London   Madrid   Milan   Munich   Paris   Montreal   Toronto
Delhi   Mexico City   Sao Paulo   Sydney   Hong Kong   Seoul   Singapore   Taipei   Tokyo

Vice President and Editor in Chief: Jeffery W. Johnston
Acquisitions Editor: Meredith D. Fossel
Editorial Assistant: Nancy Holstein
Vice President, Director of Marketing: Quinn Perkson
Senior Marketing Manager: Darcy Betts Prybella
Senior Managing Editor: Pamela D. Bennett
Senior Project Manager: Mary M. Irvin
Senior Operations Supervisor: Matt Ottenweller
Senior Art Director: Diane Lorenzo
Cover Designer: Diane Ernsberger
Cover Art: SuperStock
Composition: Aptara®, Inc.
Printer/Binder: Bind-Rite Graphics
Cover Printer: Lehigh-Phoenix Color
Text Font: Berkeley

Credits and acknowledgments borrowed from other sources and reproduced, with permission, in this textbook appear on appropriate page within text.

Every effort has been made to provide accurate and current Internet information in this book. However, the Internet and information posted on it are constantly changing, so it is inevitable that some of the Internet addresses listed in this textbook will change.

Library of Congress Cataloging-in-Publication Data
Stone, Carolyn B.
  School counselor accountability : a measure of student success / Carolyn B. Stone, Carol A. Dahir.—3rd ed.
    p. cm.
  ISBN-13: 978-0-13-704565-5
  ISBN-10: 0-13-704565-4
  1. Educational counseling—United States. 2. Educational change. 3. Education—Standards—United States.
I. Dahir, Carol A. II. Title.
  LB1027.5.S787 2011
  371.40973—dc22   2009053088

10 9 8 7 6 5 4 3 2 1

ISBN 13: 978-0-13-704565-5
ISBN 10:   0-13-704565-4

Dedication

To our family members, Elsie Bishop, Laura and Mitchell Dahir, and John Douglas Stone, and to our friends, and colleagues for their understanding of the time and commitment this project required. We would also like to dedicate this book to Jim MacGregor, Florida High School Counselor, who for two decades significantly advantaged thousands of students through his data-driven approach to school counseling. Jim represents the thousands of unsung heroes in school counseling who have been on the front lines quietly going about advantaging students by examining data to see who is being left out of the school success picture.

About the Authors

Carolyn Stone, Ed.D., is a professor at the University of North Florida (UNF) where she teaches and does research in the area of legal and ethical issues for school counselors, as well as counseling in the accountability climate. Prior to becoming a counselor educator, Stone spent 22 years with the Duval County Public Schools in Jacksonville, Florida where she served as Supervisor of Guidance, an elementary and high school counselor, and a teacher. Dr. Stone served as the President of the American School Counselor Association for the 2006–2007 school year, and currently holds the position of ASCA's Ethics Chair. She is Past-President of the Florida Counseling Association and the Florida Association of Administrators and Supervisors. Stone has delivered several hundred workshops to practicing school counselors on legal and ethical issues and working in a climate of accountability. She has written extensively on these two subjects in textbooks, journal articles, and other professional publications. She has published two textbooks: *The Transformed School Counselor* (2006, 2011) with Carol Dahir and *School Counseling Principles: Ethics and Law.*

Carolyn Stone can be contacted at UNF, COEHS, 4567 St. Johns Bluff Road South, Jacksonville, FL 32224, 904-620-1828, or by e-mail at cstone@unf.edu.

Carol A. Dahir, Ed.D., is an associate professor and the coordinator of School Counselor Education at the New York Institute of Technology (NYIT). Her career experiences include elementary school teacher, middle school counselor, and 14 years as supervisor of school counseling programs and student support services. Since 1995, Carol Dahir has consulted extensively with numerous state departments of education, school systems, school counselor associations, and national organizations on the school counseling national standards, comprehensive program development, and accountability and continuous improvement for school counselors. She is a past president of the New York State School Counselor Association, served on the governing board for the American School Counselor Association as a Vice President for Postsecondary/Supervisors, and also as the North Atlantic Region Trustee for the National Career Development Association.

An accomplished national and international presenter, Carol Dahir is the co-author of ASCA's *Sharing the Vision: The National Standards for School Counseling Programs* and *Vision into Action: Implementing the National Standards*. She has collaborated with Dr. Carolyn Stone to publish *The Transformed School Counselor* (2006, 2011) and two previous editions of *School Counselor Accountability: A MEASURE of Student Success* (2005; 2007). She writes extensively about school counselors and accountability, school improvement, and program development in textbooks, journals, and professional publications.

Carol Dahir can be contacted at NYIT, School of Education, 1855 Broadway, New York, NY 10023, 212-261-1529 or by e-mail at cdahir@nyit.edu or caroldahir@aol.com

Preface

Accountability in education evolved throughout the 1990s, eventually becoming a cornerstone of the No Child Left Behind Act (2001). Not to be left behind, a group of school counseling professionals, through the initiation of Patricia Martin and Reese House of the Education Trust, met in 2001 to discuss an accountability plan for school counselors. The collective thoughts and concerns of this group of professionals expressed the need to develop a "measurable" process that provides school counselors with a way to align their work with the accountability requirements of No Child Left Behind and the goals of school improvement. Shortly after, the American School Counselor Association's National Model (2003, 2005) prominently positioned accountability as one of the four quadrants of a comprehensive school counseling program. Since that time more than 40 state departments of education and/or school counselor associations have placed school counselor accountability at the forefront of their comprehensive school counseling models. The six step MEASURE process is a cornerstone for state models in Connecticut, Florida, Massachusetts, New York, Rhode Island, Tennessee, and Wisconsin; is used extensively in all 50 states; has been translated into Japanese; and has been introduced to counselors in Iceland, Singapore, Turkey, and the Philippines.

NEW TO THIS EDITION

School counselor accountability and the use of data-informed practice is one of the four quadrants of the ASCA National Model. Data-informed practice is highlighted in the new School Counseling Specialty Standards (Council for Accreditation for Counseling and Related Educational Programs, 2009), and is an important component of the Transforming School Counseling Initiative (Education Trust, 1997).

This new edition of School Counselor Accountability: A MEASURE of Student Success includes

- A brand new chapter on accountability and the ASCA National Model, which demonstrates to school counselors, counselors-in-training, and their professors how to fulfill the Accountability expectations of the ASCA National Model (Chapter 2–Accountability: The Cornerstone of the ASCA National Model).

- An expanded and redesigned chapter on using data, which provides school counselors with the rationale, motivation, and tips to finding, using, and analyzing data to contribute to school improvement goals (Chapter 3–Demystifying Data).

- Thirteen brand new elementary, middle, and high school MEASURES which show how individual school counselors collaborated with colleagues to positively impact a critical data element to help more students succeed (Chapter 5–School Counselors Demonstrating Accountability).

- An expanded section on school district systems and how district supervisors approach implementing MEASURE. This section demonstrates that MEASURE can have a powerful impact on systems as well as in individual schools (Chapter 5–School Counselors Demonstrating Accountability).

- A new chapter on applications of MEASURE in various masters level school counseling courses, including introductory classes, research, and internship. Counselor educators share their suggestions, assignments, and sample projects that also emphasize collaborative university-school partnerships (Chapter 6–Preparing Graduate Students to be Data-Driven Practitioners).

- A section on the relationship of MEASURE to action research, which is the perfect tool for school counselors to show the impact specific strategies have on school improvement goals (Chapter 6–Preparing Graduate Students to be Data-Driven Practitioners).

This third edition of MEASURE will:

- Provide a step-by-step process and pathway for school counselors to implement the accountability quadrant of the ASCA model.

- Encourage school counselors to collaborate with colleagues and administrators for systemic change.

- Demonstrate a simple step-by-step process for school counselors to connect their work with the expectations of school improvement and the accountability agenda of 21st-century schools.

- Encourage school counselors to engage in data-driven decision-making to implement comprehensive school counseling programs.

- Promote action research as an important vehicle for school counselors to demonstrate the impact of their work.

- Connect school counseling to the instructional program and to students' academic success.

- Reinforce the importance of school counselor skills in leadership, social justice advocacy, collaboration and teaming, use of data, and technology.

- Educate administrators, teachers, and school and community personnel to better understand how the work of school counselors contributes to the goals of school improvement.

School Counselor Accountability: A MEASURE of Student Success provides school counselors, counselor educators, graduate students, school administrators, and faculty and staff with the knowledge and skills to use data-informed practice to connect school counseling programs to school improvement. School counselors learn how to lead, advocate, collaborate and team with colleagues for the ultimate goal of improving student achievement and student success in school. MEASURE is an action research model, which describes and provides strategies for building accountability standards into counseling programs. The MEASURE process aligns school counselor led, systemic initiatives with the **accountability** component of the ASCA National Model (2003, 2005), their building and systems' goals for school improvement, and the requirements of state and national standards as well as of initiatives such as No Child Left Behind.

ACKNOWLEDGEMENTS

We would like to thank the thousands of school counselors across this country whose dedication and perseverance while improving the school experience for their students inspired and encouraged us to write MEASURE, and to those countless supervisors of school counseling and guidance who have supported the school counselors of their districts to develop and implement MEASURES. Counselor educators across the nation have used MEASURE to train the next generation of school counselors to engage in action research and use data-driven decision making to inform comprehensive school counseling program development.

A special note of appreciation is extended to the contributing school counselors who generously gave hours for meetings, phone calls, data collecting, and editing. These counselors understand the importance of accountability, and their work helps guide us to better measure school counselors' contributions to student academic success:

Scherrie Anderson, La Vergne High School; Bridget Anderson, East Hampton Middle School; Joan Apellaniz, High School for Media and Communications, George Washington Educational Campus; Dr. Dan Bullara, Mt. View Elementary School; Earnestine Benton, Westside Middle School; Michelle Brantley, school counselor at Ocee Elementary School; Sandy Braun, Executive Director, New York State School Counselor Association, Dr. Barbara A. Donnellan, Lindenhurst High School, Annie Grays, Sheffield Elementary School; Joy Guss, John Overton Comprehensive High School; Melissa Freeman, Centennial High School; Lynn Haldaman, Sweet Apple Elementary School; Emily Jenkins, Westmoreland Elementary School; Dr. Dawna K. Jenne, Kiley Middle School; Gail Leysath, Dr. Freddie Thomas High School; Dr. Rose A. Paolino, West Haven High School; Dwight Porter, Coordinator of Guidance and Counseling, Atlanta Public Schools; and Margaret Wynne, Forest Park Middle School.

We applaud the efforts of the supervisors of school counseling programs who have focused their efforts on systemic change and school counselor accountability to improve the academic success of every student in their care and who have so generously contributed the efforts of their counselors in Chapter 5, in the section on School District MEASUREs:

Yolanda D. Johnson, Director of Student Support Services, and Sonia Dinnall, Acting Supervisor of Student Support Services, Springfield Public Schools; Leigh Bagwell and Karen Meador, Student Services Counselor Liaisons, Rutherford County; Marilyn Rengert and Marnie Grimell, Program Associates, Counseling Department, Student Services, Salem-Keizer Public Schools; Kim Traverso, Central Office Education Consultant, Connecticut Technical Schools; and Dr. Bonnie J. Rubenstein, Director of School Counseling, Rochestet City Schools.

We are grateful to our counselor educator colleagues: Dr. Tina Anctil, Portland State University; Dr. Roselind Bogner, Niagra University; Dr. Joy Burnham, University of Alabama; Dr. Patricia W. De Barbieri, Southern Connecticut State University; Dr. Andrew Finch, Vanderbilt University; Dr. Hattie Isen, Cambridge College and Dr. Robert Rotunda, NYIT, Dr. Melissa Luke, Syracuse University; Patricia Landers and Delia Adorno, Central Connecticul State University; Dr. Erin Mason, De Paul University;

Dr. Karen Mackie, Assistant Professor, Counselor Education, Warner School of Education, University of Rochester; and Dr. Ellen Slicker, Middle Tennessee State University, who so generously shared their time and their experiences of using MEASURE as a collaborative model for practitioners and graduate students.

We would like to recognize Nancy Aleman, Connecticut State Department of Education; Nicole Cobb, Tennessee Department of Education; Jackie Melendez, Georgia Department of Education; Zelda Rogers, Florida Department of Education; Gary Spear, Wisconsin Department of Public Instruction; and June Tremain, Oregon Department of Education, for their vision and support of disseminating MEASURE on a statewide level.

Also to the School Counselor Associations in Connecticut, Florida, Massachusetts, New York, Rhode Island, Tennessee, and Wisconsin, for adapting MEASURE to support the accountability component of their state school counselor association models; and to Robert Tyra, Los Angeles County Education Office, for permission to adapt the Student Personnel Accountability Report Card (SPARC) to complement the Educate step of MEASURE. Their involvement and commitment to school counselor accountability significantly strengthened the impact of this work.

A special thank you to graduate students Tiffany Singleton, Reina Jovin, Kristina Zemaityte and Nathan Levinton for their research and technological assistance.

We thank the reviewers of our manuscript for their insights and comments: Ronica D. Arnold, Jackson State University; Virginia S. Dansby, Middle Tennessee State University; Mary J. Didelot, Purdue University, Calumet Campus; Susan Halverson-Westerberg; Pennsylvania State University; Susan Norris Huss, Bowling Green State University; and David C. Taylor, Central Michigan University.

In addition, we wish to express thanks to Meredith Fossel, our editor, for her constant support and encouragement and for believing in our vision of delivering a process and tool to school counselors to connect them to the goals of school improvement and share accountability for student success.

Finally we wish to thank Norman Gysbers, Curly Johnson, Patricia Martin, and Robert Myrick, trailblazers in the field of school counseling, whose contributions provided solid pathways to a bright future.

Carolyn Stone and Carol Dahir

Brief Contents

Contents

CHAPTER 4   MEASURE: Six Steps to Improving Student Success   29

CHAPTER 5   School Counselors Demonstrating Accountability   43

CHAPTER 1

The Accountability Imperative for School Counselors

ACCOUNTABILITY: EVERY EDUCATOR'S CHALLENGE

"We need to know more than what your time-on-task numbers show. Tell us how your school counseling programs impacted student success in your schools. Test scores are down, attendance is not improving, postsecondary enrollment rates are stagnant, and the end-of-year failure rate for students in Grades 4, 8, and 9 is over 35%. We appreciate our school counselors and understand that they work very hard. The numbers I have here in my hand are impressive. You delivered 2,300 classroom guidance lessons, conducted 180 groups, and made innumerable individual contacts with student and parents. We face a dire budget next year. We want to help you, but where is the justification for continuing to fund school counselors when other educators who have shown their

impact on student achievement are losing their jobs? We applaud your efforts, but in these fiscally dismal times we are forced to make tough choices. How do you know you made a difference in student achievement? Where is the data to show that your efforts have made a difference in student learning?"

—A school board member responding to the Supervisor of Guidance about tough decisions made while balancing a tight budget

START WITH STUDENT OUTCOME DATA

This all-too-real challenge from the district school board is a wake-up call for school counselors to rethink their traditional methods of demonstrating accountability. School board members, administrators, and others who are charged with making tough decisions about spending may not understand the relationship between the work of school counselors and student achievement. School counselors have not been held to the same accountability standards as other educators and have rarely been included in the conversations about how their contributions positively affect every student's academic life. Teachers and administrators have to show that they are making a positive difference in the critical data elements that school boards, legislators, parents, educators, and other community members consider to be vitally important, such as test scores, attendance, retention, dropout rates, grades, and success in rigorous academics. School counselors are just now beginning to understand how they too must be part of the discussion of how their contributions impact critical data elements. School counseling programs must start with student outcome data and then decide which data they want to track and drive in a positive direction. Once that is accomplished, the program components come into play to move the data. In other words, data is the engine that drives the school counseling program.

TIME-ON-TASK DATA

Time-on-task data needs assessments and the reporting of totals for the different types of activities are traditional school counselor demonstrations of accountability (Gysbers & Henderson, 2000). These methods of data collection are still valuable to the school counseling profession but stop short of answering the critical question of how our work affects student achievement. Gysbers and Henderson revised their work to include student impact data (Gysbers & Henderson, 2006). In recent years concerted efforts have been made to assess the effectiveness of school counseling on academic success (Campbell & Brigman, 2005; Poynton, Carlson, Hopper, & Carey, 2006) as well as the impact of comprehensive school counseling programs on academic achievement (Lapan, Gysbers, & Petroski, 2001; Lapan, Gysbers, & Sun, 1997; Sink, Akos, Turnbull, & Mvududu, 2008; Sink & Stroh, 2003).

Totaling the number of student contacts made, group sessions held, and classroom guidance lessons delivered is valuable information to let us know where we are spending our time and can help us with planning. However, this information does not have the same meaning to legislators, school board members, and other critical stakeholders. In other words, what do these totals really mean in the final analysis if groups of students are left out of the academic success picture? We must demonstrate to our stakeholders that we are powerful contributors to school improvement. Counting what we do is not enough.

How would it look, and how incredulous would stakeholders feel, if the "fire" to which teachers', principals', and superintendents' feet were held involved only time-on-task numbers?

Dear Teacher:
It is time to submit your accountability report.
To do this, answer these questions:
1. How many students did you teach this year?
2. How many lessons did you deliver?
3. How many tests did you give?
4. How many students received your one-on-one instruction?
5. How many times did you stay after school to help students?
6. How many parent conferences did you hold?
If your numbers are impressive, you pass the accountability test.

Sincerely,
Your Principal

Dear Principal:
It is time to submit your accountability report. To do this, answer these questions about your work this year:
1. How many teachers did you serve as curriculum leader?
2. How many students did you serve as principal?
3. How many Parent Teacher Association meetings did you attend?
4. How many parent conferences did you hold?
5. How many student conferences did you conduct?
6. How many teachers did you conference with this year?
If your numbers are impressive, you pass the accountability test, and your principalship is safe for another year.

Sincerely,
Your Superintendent

Dear School Counselor:
It is time to submit your accountability report. To do this, answer these questions:
1. How many classroom guidance lessons did you deliver?
2. How many students received your individual counseling services?
3. How many small groups did you deliver?
4. How many parent conferences did you conduct?
If your numbers are impressive, you pass the accountability test.

Sincerely,
Your Principal

Are these three scenarios realistic? Are teachers, principals, and superintendents allowed to count services delivered or time-on-task data as measures of accountability? Would such evaluation of effectiveness be desirable for school improvement? The answer is a resounding, "No." For these educators the question is not, "How much do you do?" but, "How are students better off academically because of what you do?" Nevertheless, school counselors have, for most of the history of our profession, counted services delivered as a primary measure of accountability. Time-on-task data is useful, but without student impact data, time-on-task numbers are inadequate measurements for all other educators, including school counselors!

RESULTS-BASED ACCOUNTABILITY

Results-based evaluation of school counseling strategies was developed by Johnson and Johnson (1991; Johnson, Johnson, & Downs, 2006) and monitors student acquisition of competencies that are needed to succeed in school, postsecondary education, and on into the work force. Results-based data document outcomes.

Needs Assessments, Surveys, Pre- and Post-Tests

Dear Teacher:
It is time to submit your accountability report.
To do this, answer these questions:
1. Did you give a needs assessment this year to see what your students were interested in learning? Did you implement the desires expressed by students in those needs assessments?
2. Did you give a pre-test and post-test following each lesson you delivered? Did your students pass your post-tests?
3. Did you give an opinion survey to your students and their parents about the effectiveness of your teaching? How many students self-reported that they learned a great deal from your lessons this year?
4. How many parents positively responded that their children learned a great deal in your class this year?
If the results of these efforts are positive, you pass the accountability test.

Sincerely,
Your Principal

Dear School Counselor:
It is time to submit your accountability report.
To do this, answer these questions:
1. Did you give a needs assessment this year to see what your students and parents needed from your school counseling program? Did you implement the ideas expressed in those needs assessments?
2. Did you give a pre-test and post-test following each lesson you delivered? Did your students pass your post-tests?
3. Did you give an opinion survey to your students and their parents about the effectiveness of your school counseling program? How many students self-reported that they benefited from your school counseling program this year?
If the results of these efforts are positive, you pass the accountability test.

Sincerely,
Your Principal

These hypothetical scenarios are moving closer to the expectations of the accountability climate, yet self-reporting, surveys, needs assessments, and interim post-tests still fall short. The heat of accountability would be less intense for teachers if their measures of accountability depended on students' self-reports of what they learned or the results of post-tests following each lesson.

Although post-tests, self-reporting, surveys, and needs assessments are moving us closer to accountability, these are still soft measures of accountability and not at the level of accountability expected by stakeholders. To deem counting and results-based approaches as adequate without showing the impact of our work on school report card data places us at risk of being viewed as a poor use of financial resources in a climate of limited funding.

STUDENT OUTCOME DATA

Outcome or impact data report the direct benefit on students' critical information such as attendance, discipline referrals, grades, promotion rates, and standardized test scores. For example, if you are running a small group for children who are constantly out of school with little good reason, will their attendance improve as a result of participating in the small group session? If school attendance for the seven students in this "School Success Group" improved by 27%, then the work of the school counselor can be linked directly to a critical element in the academic success equation. If students aren't in school, they can't learn.

Which of these approaches will resonate with school board members and legislators who are looking for positive movement in school report card data?

- **Time-on-Task Report:** Six 30-minute group sessions on goal setting were conducted with seven students in a "Children of Divorce" group.
- **Results-Base:** Five of the six children received 100% on the posttest (from pretest scores of 20%, 50%, 60%, and 80%) and one improved to 90% (from 40%)
- **Student Impact Data:** Number of Ds and Fs for the seven students reduced by 29% on the report card following the six small group counseling sessions.

The shift from counting what we do to measuring our impact on critical school-based data is most powerful when we can explain and prove that the "School Success Group" was a necessary and successful intervention needed to improve a child's academic success. Reporting a positive change in attendance is the type of accountability data that has meaning and merit to school boards and certainly to a student's future. It is much more powerful than reporting that the school counselor conducted seven groups for 35 students this year. It also means that we have to view our world through a different lens. This lens is focused on the changing times and also on the changing needs of youth in complex and dynamic educational systems that have become more accountable for student results.

ACCOUNTABILITY AND SCHOOL COUNSELORS

Public perception continues to beg frequent questions such as, "What do school counselors really do? Why do we need school counselors in our schools?" These are not newly raised concerns, and school counselors have heard variations on this theme over and over again.

Accountability, as expected by our 21ˢᵗ century stakeholders, is catching fire with the school counseling profession. School counselors are accepting the responsibility of supporting academic achievement, sharing the pressures of accountability, and demonstrating the advocacy necessary to help every student succeed.

The resistance of the past usually involved the argument that counseling fosters a personal relationship with too many variables, making it impossible to measure a counselor's effectiveness or evaluate a series of services (Myrick, 2003; Schmidt, 2000). These arguments are fading away as counselors across the country are making *accountability* a byword for our profession (Kaffenberger & Young, 2007).

Despite tremendous progress, there continues to be some resistance on the part of the counseling profession. Perhaps this is because counselors believe that accountability, as we have described it, may not be possible. Understandably, it can be difficult for school counselors to see how they can use data to isolate the things they do to contribute to the students' academic success, but because these types of measurements are being used with such frequency now, the fear of data use is considerably less.

Take a moment to reflect on your personal feelings about accountability. In every counseling situation, the need to explore motivation and emotions about an issue affects a student's ability to move in a positive direction. To contribute to the accountability agenda in our schools, we need to apply the same principles to ourselves.

Accountability is not:

- the feedback you receive from your principal on your annual evaluation. This principal report is important, but accountability focuses on how student achievement has been improved by the school counselor's work on the leadership team.
- counting services delivered such as how many groups you ran, individuals you counseled, parent conferences you held
- showing how you spend your time, such as a report that 75% of your time was in direct service with students
- survey results, needs assessments, pre- and posttests.

All of these tools are important but stop short of demonstrating school counselor impact on school improvement issues.

Accountability is:

- a means of assessing the impact of the school counseling program on school improvement
- connecting our work to student outcome data

SCHOOL COUNSELOR ACCOUNTABILITY IN CONTEXT OF EDUCATIONAL REFORM

Since America 2000 (U.S. Department of Education, 1990) and Goals 2000 (U.S, Department of Education, 1994), educational requirements and expectations have demanded much more than accounting for time and tasks from all educators. Accountability is not a new idea. Today's accountability expectations emanate from No Child Left Behind (U.S. Department of Education, 2001), which requires every educator to use school-based data to demonstrate our engagement in the school mission and student achievement.

The Achievement Gap

Working within an accountability framework shows that all educators, especially school counselors, intentionally and purposefully act to close the achievement gap (Stone & Dahir, 2006). Accepting the challenge of accountability propels school counselors into a higher profile, more powerful role to challenge barriers to learning and achievement and to raise the level of expectations for those students from whom little is expected. School counselors can challenge the pervasive belief that socioeconomic status and color determine a young person's ability to learn.

Acting as agents of school and community change, counselors can create a climate where access and support for quality and rigor is the norm. In doing so, underserved and underrepresented students now have a chance to acquire the educational skills necessary to participate fully in the 21st-century economy. School counselors can form partnerships with principals and key stakeholders to embrace accountability and to promote systemic change with the express purpose of furthering the academic success of every student (Stone & Clark, 2001). Although the number of high-school graduates is projected to increase by 5% between 2003–2004 and 2016–2017 (National Center for Education Statistics [NCES], 2007), far more needs to be accomplished to guarantee each student—regardless of ethnicity, race, or income—an equitable opportunity to a quality educational experience. School counseling programs must respond to the implications of such data. Unknowingly and without ill intent, school counselors have played a central role in maintaining the status quo, supporting inequitable schools, and serving as gatekeepers in the course selection and course placement process (Hart & Jacobi, 1992; Stone & Martin, 2004). It is time to show that, within our sphere of influence, we are willing to address:

- low expectations, specifically the pervasive belief that socioeconomic status and color determine young people's ability to learn; and

- the sorting and selecting process that acts as a filter, denying access to rigorous course content to students because of low expectations.

Beliefs Inform Behaviors

As systemic change agents, we can cultivate a belief that all children are capable of achieving (Johnson, 2000). According to United States Secretary of Education, Arne Duncan, "It is a fundamental, unalterable belief that every child can learn, and a fundamental understanding of the tremendous urgency of our work" (as cited in U.S. Department of Education, 2009, para. 23). President Barack Obama, recalling a conversation he had with Duncan about the increase of students of color doing advanced placement coursework, said, "He told me that in the end, the kids weren't any smarter than they were three years ago; our expectations for them were just higher" (American School and University, 2008, para. 13).

School counselors who focus on improving student results will be a significant contributor in raising the achievement level for every student. If school counselors are committed to high expectations for all students, regardless of race, ethnicity, and socioeconomic status (SES) then every student requires the academic and life skills preparation that opens wide the door of opportunity to all options after high school, including college. Data can be used to address concerns regarding equity, access, and success that exist in both our affluent and poverty-stricken school systems. In other words, school counseling programs can seek out those pockets of students left out of the academic success picture and contribute to creating opportunities for them. Indeed, when you read the MEASUREs from real counselors in real schools later on in this book, you will see how the attitudes and beliefs of school counselors about students' abilities to learn have contributed to many more opportunities for successful school experiences.

School counselors can:

- impact student achievement;

- improve student course-taking patterns that increase access to rigorous academic work;

- raise student aspiration and motivation;

- manage and access school and community-based resources;

- motivate students to assume responsibility for their educational and career planning;

- influence the school climate to ensure that high standards are the norm in a safe and respectful environment;

- work with our principals and faculties to create safe and drug-free communities; and

- use data to effectively identify institutional and environmental barriers that can impede student success.

School Counselors and No Child Left Behind

Every one of us has been affected by the No Child Left Behind (NCLB) legislation. Congress has stated that education is a domestic priority. NCLB intends to close the achievement gap between disadvantaged students, students of color, and their peers. NCLB promotes stronger accountability for demonstrating results and expanded options for parents to seek a high-quality education experience for their children. Student progress and achievement is published annually. Mandated state reports include performance data disaggregated according to race, gender, and other criteria. This demonstrates not only how well students are achieving overall, but also depicts progress made to close the achievement gap between disadvantaged students and other groups of students.

NCLB embodies four basic principles:

1. Stronger accountability for results, which has created standards in each state determining what a child should know, specifically in reading and math in Grades 3-8. Student progress and achievement are measured according to tests based on the state's standards and given to every child, every year.

2. Expanded flexibility and local control, which have allowed for local school districts to have more options and a greater say in how federal funds are used in their schools to meet student needs.

3. Expanded options for parents of children from disadvantaged backgrounds whose children are trapped in failing schools; providing funds to students in failing schools to use for supplemental educational services, including tutoring, after-school services, summer school programs, and charter schools.

4. An emphasis on teaching methods that have been proven to work, strengthening teacher quality, and promoting English proficiency.

NCLB has five primary goals (Fig. 1.1) that are the foundation for this national educational agenda, which extends to the school year 2013–2014. The first three goals focus on the improvement of curricula, learning, achievement and qualified personnel. Goal 4 addresses affective development, the other side of student report cards, which is the aspect of student achievement and success that takes into consideration students' personal-social development, school climate, aspiration, and motivation. Goal 5 focuses on a national crisis, i.e., improving the graduation rate in every state across our nation.

FIGURE 1.1 No Child Left Behind (2001) Elementary and Secondary Education Act

GOAL 1: By 2013–2014, all students will reach high standards, at a minimum attaining proficiency or better in reading/language arts and mathematics.

GOAL 2: All limited-English-proficient students will become proficient in English and reach high academic standards, at a minimum attaining proficiency or better in reading/language arts and mathematics.

GOAL 3: By 2005–2006, all students will be taught by highly qualified teachers.

GOAL 4: All students will be educated in learning environments that are safe, drug free, and conducive to learning.

GOAL 5: All students will graduate from high school.

School counselors recognize that a comprehensive school counseling program contributes to reaching each of the five NCLB goals. School counselors, partnering with all school personnel, help ensure that schools are safe, drug-free learning communities. Counselors also focus their efforts on creating a climate of respect among students, faculty, and community. The intent of NCLB is to ensure that every child receives an equitable education. As social justice advocates, school counselors share the same goal.

The comprehensive school counseling program contributes to Goals 1, 2, 4, and 5 in more ways that we can imagine. On a daily basis, school counselors affect the instructional program, which is the heart and soul of the education system. We encourage students to set goals and seek extra help; we collaborate with teachers to develop strategies to help at-risk students and slow learners to achieve at a faster rate; we consult with parents and support them with ideas to help their child with homework. Raising aspirations, helping students to see a bright future, and motivating students to access higher level academic courses are a significant part of the day-to-day work of the school counselor. School counselors also are ideally situated to influence Goals 4 and 5. We share the pressures of school accountability by motivating students to achieve at their highest level of ability to have all options after high school. School counselors advocate for every student to experience school success in a safe and respectful environment (Goal 4), and we work diligently toward the goal of ensuring that every child graduates from high school, regardless of the level at which we work (Goal 5).

RESPECTING TRADITION AND EXPLORING THE FUTURE

Since the early 1980s, Gysbers and Henderson (2000) and Myrick (2002) have written extensively about redesigning school counseling programs in a comprehensive and developmental format. Social pressures and the emphasis on educational student support have reframed school counseling from individual student response and crisis intervention to a proactive series of strategies that engage every student. As a result, many new models for program design and delivery systems were developed at the state and local levels in the early 1990's.

Despite these new models, the traditional viewpoint persisted, and school counselors continued to deliver an array of responsive and reactive activities that serviced a small percentage of the student population. School counseling research studies examined the professional school counselor role, analyzed time and tasks, and explored the impact and significance of interventions and prevention initiatives. Commissioned reports of national significance, such as *Keeping the Options Open* (Commission on Precollege Guidance and Counseling, 1986, 1992) and *High Hopes, Long Odds* (1994), praised school counselors for the work they do, condemned them for what they don't do, and accused school counselors of not appropriately contributing to the academic success of students. School counselors were accused of being gatekeepers, perpetuating the accepted rules and systematic barriers that cause inequities between achievers and nonachievers, based on race and socioeconomic status (Hart & Jacobi, 1992).

Throughout the 1980s and the 1990s school counseling was conspicuously absent in all the school reform efforts to promote higher levels of educational excellence. The continued omission of school counseling from the educational reform agenda was the impetus for the American School Counselor Association's (ASCA) action to advocate for the establishment of school counseling programs as an integral component of the educational system. The development of the *National Standards for School Counseling Programs* (ASCA, 1997) was an important first step in engaging school counselors and stakeholders in a national conversation about the attitudes, knowledge, and skills, in academic,

career, and personal-social development that every student should acquire as a result of participating in the school counseling program (see Appendix B). The national standards, linked to the mission of the school, encouraged school counselors to evaluate and assess the impact of their program on student achievement and school success. Most important, the standards connected school counseling to the national school reform agenda of the 1990s (Campbell & Dahir, 1997). School counselors began to see themselves as key players in preparing students to meet the increasingly complex societal demands that require significant knowledge and skills to succeed in the 21st-century. Taking a position on important educational issues, behaving as a systemic change agent, and advocating for change and continuous improvement was beginning to be the norm for school counselors (Clark & Stone, 2000).

The *National Model: A Framework for School Counseling Programs* (ASCA, 2003, 2005; see Appendix C) emphasized the importance of school counselors delivering accountable school counseling programs that carefully consider local demographic needs and the political climate of the community. The *National Model* (ASCA, 2003) speaks to the importance of having an accountability system and an organizational framework that documents how students are different as a result of the school counseling program.

The transformed 21st-century school counselor avoids working in isolation and is part of the team, contributing to the school climate and the achievement of identified student goals and outcomes, and sharing accountability for student success (Stone & Dahir, 2006).

TODAY'S CHILDREN AND THE SCHOOL COUNSELING PROGRAM

Students present a myriad of needs stemming from poverty, family dysfunction, prejudice, and learning disabilities. In contemporary society, every child is at risk of some aberrant behavior. Societal influence is strong. Violence, gangs, suicide, child abuse, teen pregnancy, substance abuse, date rape, homelessness, hunger, and lack of access to postsecondary education lurk in every community and across all socio-economic boundaries. Reflect on the following data for a minute:

The State of America's Children 2009

Key Facts About American Children:
- Every second a public school student is suspended.
- Every 11 seconds a high school student drops out.
- Every 19 seconds a child is arrested.
- Every 32 seconds a baby is born into poverty.
- Every 40 seconds a child is confirmed as abused or neglected.
- Every minute a baby is born to a teen mother.
- Every 4 minutes a child is arrested for a drug offense.
- Every 7 minutes a child is arrested for a violent crime.
- Every 18 minutes a baby dies before his or her first birthday.
- Every 45 minutes a child or teen dies from an accident.
- Every 3 hours a child or teen is killed by a firearm.
- Every 5 hours a child or teen commits suicide.
- Every 6 hours a child is killed by abuse or neglect.

Each Day in America:
- 4 children are killed by abuse or neglect.
- 5 children or teens commit suicide.
- 9 children or teens are killed by firearms.
- 32 children or teens die from accidents.
- 202 children are arrested for violent crimes.
- 377 children are arrested for drug crimes.
- 1,210 babies are born to teen mothers.
- 2,175 children are confirmed as abused or neglected.
- 2,222 high school students drop out.
- 2,692 babies are born into poverty.
- 4,435 children are arrested.
- 18,493 public school students are suspended.
  (Source: Children's Defense Fund, 2009.)

Today's school counselor shows how much he/she cares by instilling the resiliency and coping skills in children that are necessary for successful completion of the school year. The traditional way of working no longer produces the results needed to address the magnitude of societal and achievement challenges facing our students. All children and adolescents live more complicated emotional, social, academic, and technological lives than children of 10 years ago. Working individually and not systemically risks leaving huge numbers of these students, all of whom need us, out of the success picture. Our imperative is to try to meet the needs of the greatest number of students in our charge. NCLB constantly reminds us to carefully think and rethink about results and how we can influence our practice and programs.

The accountable school counseling program, now aligned with the educational enterprise, is data driven, proactive and preventive in focus, and assists students in acquiring and applying lifelong learning skills. School counseling in the 21st-century is continually moving forward, seeking ways to better serve the needs of our students and our schools, while not losing sight of our rich history and our purpose as counselors in schools.

REFERENCES

American School and University. (2008). *Duncan's priority: Reworking No Child Left Behind.* Retrieved August 12, 2009, from http://asumag.com/dailynews/edsecy/

American School Counselor Association. (1997). *The national standards for school counseling programs.* Alexandria, VA: Author.

American School Counselor Association. (2003). *American School Counselor Association national model: A framework for school counseling programs.* Alexandria, VA: Author.

American School Counselor Association. (2005). *American School Counselor Association national model: A framework for school counseling programs* (2nd ed.). Alexandria, VA: Author.

Campbell, C., & Brigman, G. (2005). Closing the achievement gap: A structured approach to group counseling. *Association for Specialists in Group Work, 30*(1), 67–82.

Campbell, C., & Dahir, C. (1997). *Sharing the vision: The national standards for school counseling programs.* Alexandria, VA: American School Counselor Association.

Children's Defense Fund. (2008). *The state of America's children: Yearbook 2008.* Washington, DC: Author.

Clark, M., & Stone, C. (2000). Evolving our image: School counselors as educational leaders. *Counseling Today, 42*(11), 21–22, 29, 46.

Commission on Precollege Guidance and Counseling. (1986). *Keeping the options open: Recommendations*. New York: College Entrance Examination Board.

Gysbers, N. C. & Henderson, P. (2000). *Developing and managing your school guidance program* (3rd ed.). Alexandria, VA: American Counseling Association.

Gysbers, N. C., & Henderson, P. (2006). *Developing & managing your school guidance and counseling program* (4th ed.). Alexandria, VA: American Counseling Association.

Hart, P. J., & Jacobi, M. (1992). *From gatekeeper to advocate: Transforming the role of the school counselor.* New York: College Entrance Examination Board.

Johnson, C. D., & Johnson, S. K. (1991). The new guidance: A system approach to pupil personnel programs. *CACD Journal, 11,* 5–14.

Johnson, L. S. (2000). Promoting professional identity in an era of educational reform. *Professional School Counseling, 4,* 31–40.

Johnson, S., Johnson, C., & Downs, L. (2006). Building a results-based student support program. Boston, MA: Houghton Mifflin/Lahaska Press.

Kaffenberger, C., & Young, A. (2007). *Making data work,* Alexandria, VA: American School Counselor Association.

Lapan, R. T., Gysbers, N. C., & Petroski, G. F. (2001). Helping seventh graders be safe and successful: A statewide study of the impact of comprehensive guidance and counseling programs. *Journal of Counseling and Development, 79,* 320–330.

Lapan, R. T., Gysbers, N. C., & Sun, Y. (1997). The impact of more fully implemented guidance programs on the school experiences of high-school students: A statewide evaluation study. Journal of Counseling & Development, 75, 292–302.

Lilly Endowment. (1994). *High hopes, long odds.* Chicago: Public Policy Research Consortium and the Indiana Youth Institute.

Myrick, R. D. (2002). *Developmental guidance and counseling: A practical approach* (4th ed.). Minneapolis, MN: Educational Media.

Myrick, R. D. (2003). Accountability: Counselors count. *Professional School Counseling, 6*(3), 174–179.

National Center for Education Statistics. (2007). *Projections of education statistics to 2016.* Retrieved August 12, 2009, from http://nces.ed.gov/programs/projections/projections2016/sec3b.asp#figf

Poynton, T. A., Carlson, M. W., Hopper, J. A., & Carey, J. C. (2006). Evaluation of an innovative approach to improving middle school students' academic achievement. *Professional School Counseling, 9*(3), 190–196.

Schmidt, J. (2000). *Counseling in schools: Essential services and comprehensive programs.* Boston, MA: Allyn & Bacon.

Sink, C., Akos, P., Turnbull, R., & Mvududu, N. (2008). An investigation of comprehensive school counseling programs and academic achievement in Washington state middle schools. *Professional School Counseling, 12*(1), 43–53.

Sink, C. A., & Stroh, H. R. (2003). Raising achievement test scores of early elementary school students through comprehensive school counseling programs. *Professional School Counseling, 6,* 352–364.

Stone, C. B., & Clark, M. (2001). School counselors and principals: Partners in support of academic achievement. *National Association of Secondary School Principals Bulletin, 85*(624), 46–53.

Stone, C., & Dahir, C. (2006). *The transformed school counselor.* Boston, MA: Houghton Mifflin/Lahaska Press.

Stone, C., & Martin, P. (2004). Data-driven decision-makers. *ASCA School Counselor, 41*(3), 10–17.

U.S. Department of Education. (1990). *America 2000: An education strategy.* Washington, D.C.: U.S. Department of Education.

U.S. Department of Education. (1994). *Goals 2000: The Educate America act.* Washington, DC: Author.

U.S. Department of Education. (2001). *No child left behind* (ERIC Document No. ED 447 608). Washington, DC: Author.

U.S. Department of Education. (2009). *Remarks of Arne Duncan to the National Education Association—Partners in reform.* Retrieved August 12, 2009, from http://www.ed.gov/news/speeches/2009/07/07022009.html

CHAPTER 2

Accountability: The Cornerstone
of the ASCA National Model

"Professional school counselors implement a comprehensive school counseling program that promotes and enhances student achievement...(¶ 1). Professional school counselors serve a vital role in maximizing student achievement. Incorporating leadership, advocacy and collaboration, professional school counselors promote equity and access to opportunities and rigorous educational experiences for all students" (¶ 2).

— *(American School Counselor Association, 2004)*

- Moving to an Accountability Mindset
- The ASCA National Model
- Foundation
- Delivery
  - Individual student planning
  - School counseling/Guidance curriculum
  - Responsive services
  - System support
- Management
- Accountability

MOVING TO AN ACCOUNTABILITY MINDSET

> *Vision without action is meaningless.*
>
> *(Spinetta, 2002, p. 24)*

For more than 25 years the professional literature has called repeatedly for increasing counselor accountability (Gysbers, 2004). Federal, state, and local expectations demand evidence-based outcomes as criteria for best practices. Accountability, as defined by *No Child Left Behind (2001)*, requires a systematic collection and analysis of key data to understand, contribute to, and improve student achievement.

In this climate of limited educational funding and the pressures of meeting "adequate yearly progress",

school counselors continue to be at risk as ancillary to the central goals of education, i.e., teaching and learning. If the work of school counselors is not aligned with these accountability expectations, policy makers, school boards and school system leaders, who are held accountable for improved results, may view the counseling programs in schools as fiscally irresponsible and as a poor use of resources (Whiston, 2002).

Since the late 1990s, school counseling has progressed from the tradition of a responsive services focus to a proactive programmatic system that is inextricably integrated with the mission of schools. The ASCA National Standards (ASCA, 1997; Campbell & Dahir, 1997), the Transforming School Counseling Initiative (Education Trust, 1997), and now the ASCA National Model: A Framework for School Counseling Programs (ASCA 2003, 2005) have directed school counselors to respect the past, embrace the present, and forge a new vision for the future. The challenges facing students and 21st-century schools have influenced the paradigms and practices that reinvigorate the profession with a renewed emphasis on supporting student achievement, social justice advocacy, and school counselor accountability.

The ASCA National Model integrated the work of Gysbers and Henderson (2000, 2006), Johnson & Johnson (2001, 2003), and Myrick (1997, 2003), added the content of the ASCA National Standards (1997) and the process skills of the Transforming School Counseling Initiative (1997). The Model integrated these four paradigms into one conceptual framework with four quadrants. The foundation, management, and delivery systems, and a new significant emphasis on accountability aligned the comprehensive program with the expectations of 21st-century schools. The Model offered the mechanism with which school counselors and school counseling teams design, coordinate, implement, manage, and evaluate their programs for students' success. The integration of these four program components with the transformed skills of advocacy, leadership, collaboration, teaming, the use of data, and the art and science of counseling, resulted in the development of the ASCA National Model.

Sadly, not all school counselors have aligned data-informed practice and accountability with equity and improving student achievement. Some continue to adhere to the "bean counting" method of accountability by reporting the totals for different types of activities. Considered "so what" data in the eyes of legislators, school board members and other critical stakeholders, this may be construed as merely a mechanism to account for productivity. School board members, administrators, and teachers, understand the difference between reporting how time is spent and demonstrating impact on academic outcomes (Louis, Jones, & Barajas, 2001; Thorn & Mulvenon, 2002; Myrick, 2003; Stone, 2003; Schmoozer, 2006).

Without a shift in thinking to the use of data to address equity issues, one cannot realize the goals of the ASCA National Model. A social justice mindset is the mantra of 21st-century practice (Stone & Dahir, 2007). In contrast to past decades, today's school counselors are expected to align their work with their building and district school improvement goals to help every student meet the expectations of higher academic standards and to contribute to closing the achievement, opportunity, and information gaps (Dahir & Stone, 2007).

The development of the American School Counselor Association (ASCA) National Standards (Campbell & Dahir, 1997) encouraged school counselors to think in terms of the expected results of what students should know and be able to do as a result of implementing a standards-based, comprehensive school counseling program. In a parallel framework, The Education Trust's De-Witt Wallace Readers-Digest Transforming School Counseling Initiative (1997) brought forward new vision skills for school counselors that emphasized leadership, advocacy, use of data, collaboration and teaming, and a commitment to support high levels of student achievement.

ASCA collaborated with the Education Trust to infuse these new vision themes of the Transforming School Counseling Initiative throughout the ASCA National Model: A Framework for School Counseling Programs in 2003. The 21st-century focus is intentional and purposeful and has at its core the belief that all children will succeed.

This collaboration sent a clear message to the profession, i.e., school counselors are ideally situated in schools to serve as social justice advocates to eliminate the achievement gap and focus their efforts on ensuring success for every underserved and underrepresented student (Hart & Jacobi, 1992; House & Martin, 1998; House & Hayes, 2002; Stone & Dahir, 2006). A penchant for social justice dictates that if school counselors "embrace a will to

TABLE 1 Changing School Counseling Paradigms and Practice

Past	Present	Future
20th-Century School Counseling: Service Driven	Transformed School Counseling: New Vision Proactive Practice	21st-Century School Counseling Aligned and Integrated with the Educational Enterprise
Counseling	Counseling	Counseling
Consultation	Consultation	Consultation
Coordination	Coordination	Coordination
	Leadership	Leadership
	Advocacy	Social justice advocacy
	Teaming and collaboration	Teaming and collaboration
	Assessment and use of data	Assessment and use of data
	Technology	Technology
		Accountability
		Cultural mediation
		Systemic change agent

Through MEASURE studies, districts can demonstrate that fully implemented Comprehensive Guidance and Counseling (CGC) Programs for Pre-K through 12TH grade in Oregon increase desired student outcomes and help eliminate unwanted achievement disparities between groups of students.

Dr. June Tremain, Office of Educational Improvement and Innovation Oregon Department of Education

excellence, we can deeply restructure education in ways that will . . . release the full potential of all of our children" (Hillard, 1991, p. 31).

THE ASCA NATIONAL MODEL

The ASCA National Model provides organizational structure that consists of four quadrants: Foundation, Delivery, Management, and Accountability, which represent the key components of a 21st-century comprehensive school counseling program. The outside frame of the diagram below represents the transformed skills of leadership, advocacy, collaboration, and systemic change to help every student succeed academically. The inside of the graphic depicts the four interrelated quadrants that are the essential components of successful and effective comprehensive school counseling programs (ASCA, 2003, 2005).

Implementing the ASCA National Model may seem complex and perhaps even overwhelming. However, by starting with a social justice mindset and the accountability quadrant you will quickly realize how using data to show the impact of your program is the cornerstone of the ASCA National Model.

Each of the four quadrants is briefly summarized in table 2.

FOUNDATION

This foundation informs the development of the philosophy, vision, and the delivery of the school counseling program standards. It is the *what* of the National Model program addressing what every student should know and be able to do (ASCA, 2003 p. 22).

The National Standards for School Counseling Programs (ASCA, 1997) are based on the three domains of student development: academic, career, and personal-social development. They are the benchmarks for student acquisition of attitudes, knowledge, and skills. The following domains can be aligned with school improvement goals and student competencies that can be identified or developed to monitor student progress.

Academic Development:

- supports student success through study and test taking skills.
- contributes to improving student attendance.
- ensures students receive academic intervention support.
- assures students and families have knowledge of and access to promotion and graduation requirements.
- focuses on increased graduation rates.
- uses data informed practice to increase opportunity and promote achievement.
- supports teachers in their work with students.

Career and Postsecondary Development:

- helps students explore postsecondary options including college and career choices.
- facilitates the college application process.
- engages parents in educational and career planning for their children.

TABLE 2

Foundation	Delivery	Management	Accountability
Mission	Four Components of the Delivery System:	School Counselor and Principal Collaboration	School Improvement Process
Vision			Using Data to Inform Practice
Guiding Principles	(1) Individual Student Planning	Advisory Council Organization	Closing the Gaps
School Counseling	(2) School Counseling / Guidance Curriculum	Calendars	MEASURE Tool
Standards and Student Competencies (Academic, Career, and Social-Personal Development)	(3) Responsive Services	Annual Program	
	(4) System Support	Summary Reports	
		Program Mapping	

- helps parents to navigate the complexities of post-secondary planning.
- provides skills necessary for student success in school, community, and the world of work.
- connects career goals to educational goals.

Personal-Social Development:

- focuses on reducing disciplinary referrals and suspension rates.
- positively impacts school climate.
- helps students acquire resiliency skills.
- encourages positive character development traits.
- promotes successful student transition from grade level to grade level.
- teaches students mediation and conflict resolution skills.
- facilitates access to community resources.
- encourages positive motivation and aspiration.

Every school counselor, in collaboration with their school improvement team, can select the standards and competencies that support positive changes that will make a difference in the desired outcomes for students.

DELIVERY

School counselors provide students with a variety of activities and strategies, as well as engage faculty and students' families and caregivers in these activities to support student success in school. We deliver these services in an intentional manner to make positive impact on student outcomes, the results of which are represented in critical data. The Delivery component describes *how* the program will be implemented and defines the implementation process. The comprehensive program is delivered through four components: (1) individual student planning, (2) school counseling/guidance curriculum, (3) responsive services, and (4) system support. Every school counseling activity should be aligned with one of these four component areas.

Individual Student Planning

School counselors develop, coordinate, and monitor *Individual Student Plans* as a means of ensuring academic excellence for all students. Plans consist of the coordination of all systemic activities provided within the school setting focusing on academic, career, and personal-social development. Through individual student planning, counselors can assist students in establishing goals and monitoring and managing their own learning and behavior.

Individual Student Plans provide the structure to promote successful transition from grade level to grade level, from school to school, school to career and/or school to higher education. Individual students' plans are developed and follow the student, as needed, through all grade levels. Individual student planning can be delivered in the following ways:

- **Individual:** Meet with student to develop and monitor the plan.
- **Small Group:** Provide service delivery in a small group setting focusing on plan development, review, and implementation.
- **Classroom:** Consult with teaching staff in the development and monitoring of plans.
- **Case Management:** Monitor student progress via individual meetings with students, review of graded work, assessments and report cards, and consultation with teaching staff.
- **Crisis Intervention:** Provide responsive crisis intervention as needed to the student or via a preventative behavioral management plan.
- **Parents/Guardians:** Establish and coordinate the delivery of individual student plans and meet with the counselor and student.

Moreover, student planning occurs within the three domains of academic, career, and personal/social development.

- *Academic planning* consists of reviewing standardized test scores, i.e., PSAT, SAT, state test; developing four-year educational plans and plans for higher education; identification of strengths and weaknesses; and credit reviews (at the secondary level).

- *Career planning* consists of utilizing career assessments tools, identification of strengths and weaknesses, and the development of a post high school career and/or academic plan prior to graduation.

- *Personal-social planning* consists of identification and awareness of self and respect for others, assessment of personal management skills, development of strategies for processing feelings, emotions, problem solving, conflict resolution, and the development and monitoring of behavior management plans.

Individual student planning that is ongoing, focused, and intentional will ensure that students take hold of their academic, career, and personal-social dreams, and have the educational plan and goals to bring these to fruition.

School Counseling/Guidance Curriculum

The school counseling/guidance curriculum promotes knowledge, attitudes, and skills through instruction in three areas: academic achievement, career development, and personal-social growth. The curriculum is planned, ongoing, and systematic with units of instruction. The scope and sequence of the curriculum incorporates school improvement goals, the school counseling standards, and input from school and community stakeholders. Most importantly, the curriculum serves student needs and what teachers believe students will most benefit from. No longer can we continue to deliver the same unit on goal setting year in and year out unless there is a need supported by data.

Lessons are delivered by the following methods:

- **Classroom Instruction:** School counselors provide instruction in collaboration with classroom teachers, staff, and/or other stakeholders around topics such as motivation, getting along with others, goal setting, decision making, career and college planning, respecting self and others, peer pressure, conflict resolutions, etc. Existing curricula may also be used as part of classroom instruction.

- **Interdisciplinary Curriculum Development:** School counselors work in conjunction with staff to develop lessons which connect content areas through state and district curriculum standards and the school counseling (guidance) curriculum. Examples may include organizational and study skills, test-taking strategies, community service, etc.

- **Group Activities:** School counselors provide instruction to students in a small group setting inside (push in) or outside of the classroom. This has a different purpose than group counseling and helps to reinforce or remediate skills that students may not have acquired in a whole group lesson.

Responsive Services

This component of the Delivery System is focused on the immediate needs of individuals and groups. The school counselor uses individual and group counseling, groups, consultation, and crisis intervention to provide proactive and responsive services. Responsive services ensure appropriate and timely responses to academic, career, and personal-social concerns, and are available to every student. Services are often student-initiated through self-referral, or teachers, staff, and parents may refer students for assistance. Responsive strategies include, but are not limited to:

- **Individual Counseling:** An opportunity to identify and clarify a concern to guide a student towards individual growth.

- **Small Group Counseling:** Group counseling that focuses on mediation and prevention issues.

- **Referral:** May be made within and/or outside the school setting for in depth and on-going counseling and therapeutic services.

- **Crisis Counseling:** Prevention, intervention, and follow-up services to students in emergency situations.

- **Conflict Resolution/Mediation:** Counselors can provide direct services to students engaged in conflict and/or train peer mediators to aid in the conflict resolution process.

These strategies, activities and services are the heart and soul of the school counseling program. No longer is it enough to provide individual and group counseling for its own sake. It is much more powerful in your accountable, comprehensive program to show how working with a group of 3rd grade students, who are struggling to pay attention in class,

SCHOOL COUNSELOR LEADERSHIP AND SYSTEM SUPPORT AT KILEY MIDDLE SCHOOL IN SPRINGFIELD, MA

Dr. Dawna K. Jenne, chairperson of the Kiley Middle School Counseling Department, and her counselors Nancy Sousa Giza and James Goodwin were committed to supporting and engaging teachers to achieve their goal of improving attendance. Together, they collaborated with administrators and teachers to address issues that impact student attendance and strategize interventions to improve attendance.

Through *System Support* they utilized team meetings, in-service, professional development, and service on key school committees to show how Kiley counselors, as does every member of the Kiley family, prides themselves on their role in helping our students succeed academically and emotionally.

has positively impacted their grades from failing to passing.

System Support

System support consists of activities that establish, maintain, and enhance the total school counseling program as a critical and effective component of the overall educational program. System support can include:

- **Professional Development:** Participation in and presentation of in-service training, membership in professional associations, and continued post-graduate education and research.

- **Consultation/Collaboration/Teaming:** Consultation and collaboration with staff, parents/guardian, and community members and organizations in order to meet student needs and provide/receive information relevant to the school counseling program. School counselors can also involve all stakeholders in these conversations and unite them around a particular goal or cause.

- **Program Management:** Planning and organizing conversations around school improvement goals, issues of equity and access, and gaps in achievement. Data analysis and data-informed practice support the activities of an accountable, comprehensive school counseling program.

- **Participation in School Committees:** School counselors serving on key school committees, especially the school improvement team.

- **Workshops and Seminars:** Planning and implementing after school and evening programs for parents, students, and faculty aimed at closing the information gap.

MANAGEMENT

The *Management* component addresses the *when*, *why*, and *on what* authority the program is delivered (ASCA, 2003 p. 22). This section also presents the organizational processes and tools needed to deliver a comprehensive school counseling program and includes:

- School Counselor and Principal Collaboration
- Advisory Council
- Organization
- Calendars
- Quarterly Reports
- Annual Program Summary Reports
- Program Mapping

Implementing these activities ensures that planning and goal setting is collaborative and meets the school's need to further every student's achievement. Utilizing a *Management* system assures input from members of the school and community, establishes a timeline for the delivery of services and programs, and serves as an organizational tool to align school counseling activities and services with the goals of school improvement.

Mapping is a process that organizes all of the activities in the comprehensive school counseling program around the four quadrants of the ASCA Model (Dahir, 2005). The Mapping process identifies grade level competencies and strategies as well as assisting with the identification of gaps in service delivery. Program mapping benefits the student and counselor by providing a comprehensive timeline for service delivery and is used to develop a Pre-K through 12 scope and sequence. Mapping can also help identify all the services in the delivery system that must include individual student planning and responsive services. It helps the school counselor understand if there is an over- or under-emphasis on critical comprehensive school counseling activities.

Without an organizational plan or, in other words, a management system, many good intentions go by the wayside and annual goals may never be achieved. A management plan is also an assurance that school counselors are focused on the same school-based goals as administrators, faculty, and staff, and that all stakeholders support the same goals for success.

ACCOUNTABILITY

You are aware that an important emphasis of the ASCA National Model is the involvement of school counselors in sharing responsibility for the improvement of student learning and academic success, as well as the implementation of strategies to narrow the achievement gap. The Foundation, Delivery and Management components establish the content and process for the program. However, it is the *Accountability* quadrant that answers the question: "How are students different as a result of the school counseling program?" The ASCA Model encourages school counselors to demonstrate accountability. When school counselors work with the same school-based data as their colleagues, they share accountability for student outcomes and contribute to moving critical data in a positive direction.

A successful school counseling program affords counselors the ability to measure the effectiveness of services so that they can then demonstrate the benefits and impact of those services, or identify ways in which the services can be improved. Each year, school counseling programs set measurable goals in the academic, career, and personal-social development domains based on data, school improvement plans, and collaboration with school and community stakeholders. To evaluate the program and demonstrate accountability, school counselors must collect and use data that links the program to both student achievement and school improvement. School counselor accountability includes measurement, data collection, decision making, and evaluation focusing on student achievement and contributing to the school and district improvement goals.

An accountable school counseling program includes the following:

- An alignment with the school Mission and school improvement process.
- Commitment to working with a critical data Element as part of program design and implementation.
- Analayzing data.
- Facilitating a Stakeholders' Unification around goals and delivery of strategies.
- Monitoring Results.

- Educating all about the results: administrators, faculty, staff, students, families, and community supporters.

Time is no longer a luxury. Ethically speaking, school counselors cannot sit back (ASCA, 2004) and watch the "gaps" grow. Data-informed design and program implementation are essential for the profession to thrive and survive in the 21st century.

Chapter 3, which follows, provides a more detailed discussion around using data, and in Chapter 4 you will be introduced to an acronym, **MEASURE**, a six-step accountability action plan that places school counselors in a leadership role to help facilitate school improvement goals.

REFERENCES

American School Counselor Association. (1997). *Executive summary: The national standards for school counseling programs.* Alexandria, VA: Author.

American School Counselor Association. (2003). *American school counselor association national model: A framework for school counseling programs.* (1st ed.). Alexandria, VA: Author.

American School Counselor Association. (2005). *American school counselor association national model: A framework for school counseling programs.* (2nd ed.). Alexandria, VA: Author.

Campbell, C., & Dahir, C. (1997). *Sharing the vision: The national standards for school counseling programs.* Alexandria, VA: American School Counselor Association.

Dahir, C. (2005). *No school counselor left behind. Aligning with the ASCA national model.* Annual Meeting of the American Counseling Association. Atlanta: GA

Dahir, C.,& Stone, C. (2007). *School counseling at the crossroads of change. ACA Professional Counseling Digests.* (ACAPCD-05). Alexandria, VA: American Counseling Association.

Education Trust (1997). *Transforming school counseling initiative. DeWitt Wallace-Reader's Digest grant.* Washington, D.C.: Author.

Education Trust. (1997). *Working definition of school counseling.* Washington, D.C.: Author.

Gysbers, N.C. (2004). *Comprehensive guidance and counseling programs: The evolution of accountability. Professional School Counseling, 8,* (1). 1–14.

Gysbers, N.C., & Henderson, P. (2006). *Developing and managing your school guidance program* (4th ed.). Alexandria, VA: American Counseling Association.

Gysbers, N.C., & Henderson, P. (2000). *Developing and managing your school guidance program* (3rd ed.). Alexandria, VA: American Counseling Association.

Hart, P., & Jacobi, M. (1992). *Gatekeeper to advocate.* New York: College Board Press.

Hillard, A. (1991). *Do we have the will to educate all children?* Educational Leadership. 48, pp. 31–36.

House, R. M., & Hayes, R. L. (2002). *School counselors: Becoming key players in school reform. Professional School Counseling, 5,* 249–256.

House, R. & Martin, P. (1998a). *Advocating for better futures for all students: A new vision for school counselors. Education, 119,* 284–286.

Johnson, C.D., & Johnson, S.K. (2001). *Results-based student support programs: Leadership academy workbook.* San Juan Capistrano, CA: Professional Update.

Johnson, C.D., & Johnson, S.K. (2003). *Building stronger school counseling programs: Bringing futuristic approaches into the present.* Greensboro, NC: Caps Publishers.

Louis, K. S., Jones, L. M., & Barajas, H. (2001). *Evaluation of the transforming school counselor initiative: Districts and schools as a context for transformed counseling roles.* Minneapolis, MN: University of Minnesota, Center for the Applied Research and Educational Improvement.

Martin, P. (1998). *Transforming School Counseling.* Unpublished manuscript. Washington, D.C.: The Education Trust.

Myrick, R.D. (1997). *Developmental guidance and counseling: A practical approach* (3rd ed.). Minneapolis, MN: Educational Media Corporation.

Myrick, R.D. (2003). *Accountability: Counselors count.* Professional School Counseling, 6, 174–179.

Schmoozer, M. (2006). *Results now.* Alexandria, VA: Association for Supervision and Curriculum Development.

Spinetta, A. (2002, October). *Where's the conversation?* Converge, 5, 24.

Stone, C. (2003). *Philosophical counselor as social justice advocate.* Journal of Canadian Philosophical Counseling. University of St. Paul: Ottawa, Canada.

Stone, C., & Dahir, C. (2004). *School counselor accountability: A measure of student success.* Upper Saddle River, NJ: Pearson Education.

Stone, C., & Dahir, C. (2006). *The transformed school counselor.* Boston, MA: Houghton Mifflin/Lahaska Press.

Stone, C., & Dahir, C. (2007). *School counselor accountability: A measure of student success.* (2nd ed.). Upper Saddle River, NJ: Pearson Education.

Thorn, A.R., & Mulvenon, S. W. (2002). *High-stakes testing: An examination of elementary counselors' views and their academic preparation to meet this challenge.* Measurement and Evaluation in Counseling and Development, 35(3), p. 195

U.S. Department of Education. (2001) *No child behind act of 2001 (H.R.1).* Washington, D.C.: U.S. Department of Education.

Whiston, S.C. (2002). *Response to the past, present, and future of school counseling: Raising some issues.* Professional School Counseling, 5, 148–155.

CHAPTER 3

Demystifying Data

Better standards. Better teaching. Better schools. Data-driven results. President Barack Obama

(Education Week, July 24, 2009)

The Obama–Biden education plan intends to restore the promise of America's public education. Every member of the school community is an important player in making this intention a reality. For too many years, school counselors worked in isolation, supporting individual students at risk or in need. Becoming part of this promise and ensuring that every child has the right to a quality and equitable education is every school counselor's ethical responsibility. Understanding and using data are essential skills school counselors need to make this happen.

DATA FIRST

The influence of business thinking on the education sector is profound. Business and education executives were reminded by Jim Collins in *Good to Great* (2001) to urge their organizations to confront the brutal facts about themselves (p. 65). In the bottom line, facts equal data. The school improvement agenda is driven by accountability!

Twenty-first century education is grounded in accountability and now is every educator's bottom line. Data-driven decision-making, or using data informed practice, is every administrator's top priority. So what do school counselors need to do?

First and foremost, school counselors simply need to understand what data is and how to use it to become major contributors to the goal of helping every child succeed and achieve. Thinking about data can be overwhelming. Data implies statistics and thousands of pages of numbers. Erase that image from your mind, (as well as that semester spent in statistics) and let's take a straight-forward and focused approach to understanding the basic principles of finding, interpreting, and applying data.

The simplest way to begin to use data is to take a careful look at your school's improvement plan and your school's report card and use this information to design and implement your comprehensive school counseling program. Just like the "chicken or the egg" debate, is it program development first or data? Consider this: data is knowledge. Knowledge is power. Thus, let's begin with a solid understanding of the critical data elements that are presented publicly about our schools in the annual report cards published and widely distributed by your state department of education. This data tells the story of your students' accomplishments and provides the facts to define real need rather than the perceived need. Once we have the facts in hand, we can develop the strategies to deliver a comprehensive school counseling program that is aligned with your school's annual improvement plan. The school counseling strategies and activities are focused on helping every one of your students succeed academically, in personal-social development, as well as in the career domain. Need we say more?

Existing school data can help you establish goals for your school counseling program. Using data to analyze patterns of behavior and student achievement provides insight into who is not succeeding. A school counseling program built around data uses facts, rather than assumptions or perceptions. Data, such as enrollments in college prep courses, graduation rates, retention rates, special education placements, attendance, grades, and standardized test scores, reveal a telling story of achievement patterns, equity issues, career and college connections, and the overall effectiveness of schools (Dahir & Stone, 2003; Martin, 2004).

WHY USE DATA?

One picture is worth a 1000 numbers!

Data paints a vivid picture of a school and its students. Our school report cards are graphic representations of the successes and failures in our buildings and systems. Critical data elements are those pieces of information that are publicly displayed as key indicators of the many factors that schools address on a daily basis. These include: attendance; promotion rates; number of suspensions; graduation rates; postsecondary going rates; standardized test results; and disciplinary incidents. Closely examining these critical data elements, which identify the needs of your students and the school-wide issues that cloud success, is the first step to inform and guide the development of an accountable school counseling program. By using data, school counselors can accurately present the current challenges their students face and highlight accomplishments in all of the critical areas. Using data to tell the story identifies the needs of your students in your caseload and across each grade level.

Examining data also reveals the school-system-wide challenges that impact success. Using data can help us visualize the end result as well as the patterns of accomplishment. Data helps us to identify and eliminate school policies and practices that may be limiting some students' ability to graduate, access higher-level academics, use school and community resources, or gain educational opportunities after high school. Understanding and using data is the school counselor's roadmap to social justice and equity.

DATA DATA EVERYWHERE

There is more data surrounding us than most of us ever want to think about; so much so, it can become overwhelming. Many school counselors have access to student management systems or databases that contain school demographic information, students' biographical information, as well as course information, student schedules, attendance, discipline, and test history.

These information systems are useful when working with students on measurables such as attendance, test scores, current grades, and past academic performance. By examining school-wide data in this way, you can be sure that no students are being left out of the picture (Dimmitt, Carey & Hatch, 2007; Martin, 2004). This provides equity in analysis and guarantees that no group of students will be left out of critical calculations for a data-driven school counseling program (Stone & Turba, 1999). It is easy to focus on what data elements you don't have rather than examining the data you are able to obtain. "Work for but don't wait for perfect data" (The Education Trust, 2001). Student report card grades and comments, discipline referrals, assessment results, and high school profiles are just a few examples of additional data that is readily available and accessible in every school building.

ASKING THE RIGHT QUESTIONS

We frequently hear the term data-driven decision-making, which describes the use of data to inform practice. Our administrators use this approach to lead their school leadership/improvement teams. But what does this mean to school counselors? Let's begin by focusing on questions, not the data. What do you want to know? What information do we need to find answers so that practice can be driven by facts not fiction? Data-driven decision-making does not simply require good data; it also requires good decisions (Hess, 2009 p. 17).

School counselors have always connected looking at the whole child and the factors that influence progress. Armed with facts (data), we can help our administrators and colleagues ask the essential questions to find the data that will help us answer our core questions. We may be data rich and have more information available to us, but we may lack the ability to sort and prioritize. In addition to the student management systems, our administrators also have access to data collected about achievement, things like report card comments, disciplinary reports, test scores, grades, and so on.

Making connections between these various data sets will help us focus on what is most important. In our school, do student outcomes differ by demographics? In our school, what is the profile of a successful student? A failing student? A dropout? What percentage of students achieved proficiency last year but did not this year? We then can use data to answer the questions that count (Ronka, Lachat, & Meltzer, 2009). Collaborative analysis can lead to collaborative action.

Let's examine an example of one school's improvement goal: by the end of the next school year, 90% of our 8th graders will achieve the proficient level designation on the annual state exam. Where do you even begin to figure out what data to look at? The amount of available data can be overwhelming: state test scores, patterns of passing and failing rates, percentages of students receiving academic support, numbers of students who are English Language Learners, and then, possibly, add student demographics including attendance, transiency, and poverty levels. How can we possibly look at all of this data, make sense of it, and create strategies and interventions? What types of data do we need, and equally important, how do we organize it in a way that is manageable? Most importantly, school counselor proficiency in collecting, disaggregating, and analyzing data is essential to better understanding and supporting student success in 21st-century schools.

DATA 101

Data can be categorized as qualitative (narrative) or quantitative (numerical). School data management systems are repositories of demographic data that describes, in quantitative form, the student body, the staff, and the community. Studying demographic data provides insight into the profile of the student body, and also can show changes over time. Demographic data is often coupled with other achievement, attendance, and behavior categories to further analyze which groups of students are succeeding and which are struggling.

> *Throughout my nine years as a school counselor, I have been in search of a way to show how the work I do impacts student achievement. MEASURE has been a huge success at my school for two years. I have seen student gains and, for the first time I am able to show the results.*
>
> (Michelle Brantley, Ocee Elementary Fulton County Georgia)

Quantitative data also include test scores, discipline referrals, retention rates, course enrollment, and attendance. Most of the examples used throughout this text are quantitative. School counselors maintain case notes, anecdotal observations, and case studies, all of which are considered qualitative data.

The ASCA National Model (2003, 2005) describes three types of data usage: process, perception, and results (impact): Process data confirms how many times an event occurred, for how long, who was involved and how the event was conducted. However, it does not provide any information as to how this strategy influenced student success as a direct result of the school counseling program. For example, as part of the school counselors' commitment to contribute to this collaborating with teachers to improve grades, every 8th grade student participated in six school counseling/guidance lessons that focused on organizational skills and study skills. The sessions were planned and delivered as a collaboration of teachers and counselors. Process data measure the

Michelle Brantley, school counselor at Ocee Elementary School in St. John's Creek, Georgia, set up her demographic profile in this manner:

Enrollment: 810 students

School Demographics:

Caucasian/Non-Hispanic: 57.41%

African American: 8.89%

Hispanic: 7.65%

Asian/Pacific Islander: 20.37%

Native American: 0.12%

Multi-Racial: 5.56%

Free-Reduced lunch: 11.24%

English as Second Language: 7.16%

Exceptional Student Education/Special Education: 13.83%

implementation of programs and the amount of time school counselors are engaged in a particular activity, such as individual counseling. The program audit, which establishes the degree of implementation of a comprehensive school counseling program, identifies areas for improvement and provides an overall view of the total program effectiveness, is another example of process data (Stone & Dahir, 2007).

Perception data is a snapshot in time that allows you to analyze changes in attitudes, beliefs, or needs over time and is often collected as pre and post information, as need assessments, or surveys. Students may be asked, "What do you know about XYZ? "and at the end of the lesson, "What do you now know about XYZ that you didn't know before?" As a result of the school counseling/guidance lesson, students have the opportunity to share their changes in attitude about studying or organizing their notes in a new way. They can respond with how they acquired new knowledge about how to organize and study, while confirming their belief that they can apply what they learned by participating in these six lessons.

It is important to remember to focus on collecting the data that is helpful to improving the desired student outcomes. We don't have to know about every student's needs or wishes because surveys and needs assessments are a snapshot in time of the perception of the moment, and those can change frequently.

Results data (Johnson, Johnson & Downs, 2006) shows impact and provides information to evaluate programs. Generally the data supports or does not support the goals of the program. For example, as a result of these 6 classroom guidance lessons, have 90% of the 8th graders improved their class work, handed in all of their homework, passed all of their classes, and ultimately improved their scores on the state test? Which indicators do we monitor? How frequently do we do this?

In summary, perception data (attitudes and beliefs) is gathered through questionnaires, needs assessments, focus groups, and interviews. School process data (occurrences) tells us about classroom techniques, specific instructional strategies, and school-wide program adoption. Results or impact data demonstrates the impact of our intervention(s).

What makes the gathering and understanding of data manageable is your ability to keep focused on the essential questions, access the data that will help find answers, monitor progress, and identify results regarding those essential questions. As the questions are discussed and organized, it becomes clear just how much data we really need to conduct a CSI (Counselor Systemic Investigation).

Descriptive Data

Let's refer back to our school improvement goal, which is about improving 8th graders' achievement on the state tests. In order to do that, we need to ask questions to discover more about our 8th grade students. Using simple descriptive statistical procedures is essential.

Descriptive data creates a comprehensive picture that reveals important information for interpretation and is the foundation for your inquiry (The Education Trust, 2006). The purpose of using descriptive statistics is to describe or summarize data in a parsimonious manner through the use of central tendency (mean, mode, and median); variability (range of an item, quartiles, quintiles, deciles, etc., and standard deviation; and relative position, which can show percentile ranks, i.e., the percentage of scores that fall at or above a given score. Descriptive statistics simply do that—they describe. Averages, percentages, mean scores, and distance from the standard deviation simply do describe the facts.

Disaggregating Descriptive Data

School counselors can learn to harness the power of aggregated and disaggregated student information. Disaggregating data, that is separating out the data by variables such as ethnicity, gender, socio-economic status, or teacher assignment, provides a picture of different sub groups. This way of first organizing your data helps us to identify the students not succeeding and then examine the subsets of the larger (aggregated) population. These subgroups can also be linked to other factors such as gender and attendance, current grades, and test scores. Student data management systems make all of this possible and eliminate the stress of manual counting.

Sagor (2005) reminds us to subdivide performance data by any categories that we suspect are relevant. Looking at the data in this manner becomes a powerful tool for identifying inequities between and among groups. It also arms school counselors with a powerful ability to develop a social justice agenda. Disaggregation makes it possible to determine how policy and practice affect issues of equity, enabling all school counselors to work closely with building administrators and faculty to close the achievement gap.

Data reveals the dissonance between what people believe, or assume is happening in schools, and reality. Remember: focus on identifying which data is related to what you want to know and what you intend to change in order to improve student success.

Longitudinal Data

Patterns over time also reveal information about student progress both for the individual and for groups. If we are curious about these trends over time, then analyzing longitudinal data, over months or years, can reveal gains and losses for the individual/group that you are analyzing.

Organizing Data

Now that we have identified what we want to look at (8th grade achievement on state test scores), we need to look at the volume of information in front of us and arrange the data in a way that allows us to find answers to the questions we have. Technological tools allow us to do data mining and data warehousing, tools that are readily available to help you organize and work with your data. Most school computers have Excel or a comparable spreadsheet system installed to help you input, disaggregate, and create charts and graphs of your data that will show your results. Many student data management systems allow information to be imported from or exported into spreadsheet systems to combine student demographic data with the elements or variables that you want to analyze.

The National Center for Education Statistics http://nces.ed.gov has a section called *Kids Zone* that walks you through how to use, organize, and chart data. Another free download, EZ*analyze* is a very user-friendly tool that links to your existing Excel spreadsheet. This tool and web site were created by Dr. Timothy Poynton, a counselor educator at Suffolk University in Massachusetts. You can access EZ*analyze* (*and it's free*) at http://www.ezanalyze.com.

THE POWER OF DATA

> *Effective data systems can "target the right services to the right schools at the right time"*
>
> *(Peltzman & Jerald, 2006, p.8)*

Data can help you better understand that you can answer almost any question about the effectiveness of your school's programs and school counseling effort on student outcomes. Data is the best tool we have for understanding the current situation in our school at any given time. Data also demonstrates how the school counseling program is contributing to overall student progress and student achievement. Data tells us about our efforts and the efficacy of our program, including the strategies or interventions that were developed and implemented. The bottom line for school counselors is that data allows us to identify and eradicate practices that may be deterring access to, or success in, higher-level academics.

The power of data resides in the knowledge that allows all schools and their students to achieve, regardless of economic factors, ethnic background, or cultural heritage. Data can be used to inform educators' decisions, not replace them (Secada, 2001). Data is a counselor's best friend. It provides new information that can be used to guide action (Light, et al., 2004). These are the central pillars of a data-informed practice.

> *I challenge my counselors regularly to create programs to address student needs and highlight data. This keeps our work relevant and helps counselors stay focused.*
>
> *(Dwight Porter, Coordinator of Guidance and Counseling, Atlanta Public Schools)*

DATA: FRIEND OR PHO-BIA

Using data often conjures up the struggles and nightmares that some of us experienced with statistical analysis in our graduate programs. We looked at pages of printouts searching for meaningful interpretations. Simple mention of "data analysis" can conjure this underlying statistical phobia, a fear that not only affects school counselors, but can also deter school administrators!

Putting complex statistical analyses aside, the effective use of data in schools relies upon simplicity. Consider this a balm to cure data-phobia: ask yourself, "Which data do we need to examine to help us better understand our students' successes and failures?" The data can tell us how many students are passing and how many are failing. Within those two categories, those who are passing, and those who are failing, we can now examine many of the factors that contribute to student success and failure.

Let's work through a scenario that can be adapted for older or younger students. This past June at Riverdale Middle School, 78% of the eighth graders passed the state exam allowing their promotion to the high school. Twenty-two percent of the student body must attend and pass summer school to move on to ninth grade. The students are upset; teachers are frustrated; and parents are complaining about their summer plans. How could this have happened? Could we have avoided this difficult situation?

Placing blame will not resolve the frustration experienced by so many of the stakeholders, especially the students. Looking for ways to reduce failure in the future is the most significant contribution the school counselors can make to the school improvement agenda. The solution may lie in examining the data to reveal the patterns of success and failure that these eighth graders experienced over the course of the school year.

Research also reminds us that establishing specific school improvement goals and implementing supportive strategies is the most important action in the school improvement process (McGonagill, 1992; Schmoker, 1999, 2001; Schmoozer, 2006). When the Riverdale Middle School improvement team convened immediately after the results arrived, every grade level/department in the school building identified strategies to improve the 8th grade math scores for the following year. Referring back to the original goal, the school improvement team determined that a school-wide effort was needed to increase the number of students passing the state exam from 78% to 90%.

MAKING CONNECTIONS

School counselors do not deliver the core subjects that are tested, so how can the school counselors contribute to this goal of improving the 8th grade state exam scores? Let's start by analyzing the information we have, so we can figure out what we need to do next.

I already know _____

I need to know _____

The next step is to reassess the situation, breaking apart the missing information into a list of further questions.

What do we want to know? What questions do we need to ask?

Who has or can help me locate the additional information that I need? _____

_____

Large-scale (aggregated) data tells me only one part of the story. In what ways can I disaggregate the data to

look for ways to improve the eighth-grade state exam scores? _____

_____

Keep It Simple

We are not looking to do complex analyses or correlation studies (Schmoker, 1999, 2001). Complexity will only lead to overload and confusion. Let's work through this problem and fill in the blanks:

I already know: that 22% of our students did not pass the state exam.

I need to know: the impact of absenteeism on student achievement and how students are performing on core academic subjects.

Who has, or can help me locate the additional information that I need? The assistant principal in charge of the student data management system; teachers from the core academic subjects departments; other members of the faculty and staff who work with the eighth graders; and talking with students who passed, and failed in the past.

Large-scale (aggregated) data tells me only one part of the story. In what ways can I disaggregate the data to look for ways of improving the 8th grade test scores? Why not start by disaggregating the data by gender, ethnicity, absenteeism, and socio-economic status?

The Next Steps

After reviewing the disaggregated data, you and the other school counselors know they can contribute to this important goal. Utilizing *system support*, you can conduct an in-service to help the teachers to better understand, not just the actual results and numbers, but also which students and groups of students fell through the cracks when problems began to surface. Many students exhibited warning signs way back in September. You and your colleagues can also address student perceptions about success, particularly in English Language Arts and math, the teachers' disappointment with the results, and the parents' frustration about their children's lack of progress. The data paints a vivid picture of which students passed and which failed. The more you can organize and analyze, the better you understand student needs and, ultimately, help the faculty improve the passing rate for this year's 8th grade state exam.

The Riverdale middle school counselors also discovered that there were no obvious differences in the performance of boys and girls. As they looked deeper into the data, they eliminated a "female math phobia" hypothesis; female students' scores on the math component of the exam were comparable to the boys' scores. It was discovered that the students who performed at the lowest level were those who were either mainstreamed from special education classes or regular education students who were labeled "slow learners." They asked each other questions; they organized the data on a spread sheet and arranged it in a way that offered insight to the questions. Finally, they shared their findings with the principal and the 8th grade teachers.

Armed with a summary that included charts and graphs, they began to connect the pieces of the puzzle to profile who successfully passed the exam and who hadn't. The teachers were not surprised at the findings; however, they were surprised that the counselors had not thought about digging deeper previously. The data revealed that this pattern of failure was not new and had occurred for several years, although not to the same degree. Together they discovered that students who failed never stayed for extra help classes after school and that the majority of the students who failed lived a great distance from the school, relying exclusively on bus transportation.

The anonymity of failure had taken on shape, form, personal characteristics and now, finally, "faces". Looking at data longitudinally also revealed that the majority of the students had extremely high absenteeism in the formative years of second and third grade. The majority of the students lagged behind their peers for years, going unnoticed until this year's abysmal 8th grade passing rate.

What a wealth of information came to light! Each piece of new data prompted the school counselors and teachers to look further. By taking initiative, the school counselors slowly and methodically peeled away the layers that revealed annually recurring phenomena that had previously gone unnoticed. Together, they were stakeholders and collaborators in the quest to help every one of their students to succeed.

This way of work might require significant changes in our practice; we might have to go an extra mile! The principal asked the counselors if they would share these findings with the 6th and 7th grade teachers also. They learned that they must begin their efforts from the 1st day their students entered the middle school. It didn't matter what grade level they worked in, every member of our school community was asked to become a stakeholder, united in a common goal—student academic success leading to a goal of a 100% passing grades on the 8th grade exam.

As part of the school improvement team, the school counselors began to establish a student profile consisting of warning signs that could lead to failure. The math teachers could now target and intervene early on in the semester and not wait until the third marking period. English Language Arts teachers planned a series of targeted activities to help students with weak reading comprehension skills. Writing contests were planned, as well as a social studies competition. Most importantly, the school improvement team also reached out to the Parent Teacher Association (PTA) to rally the parent community to attend a series of workshops focused on getting them involved with their children's homework.

Following the *Understanding by Design* process (Wiggins & McTighe, 1998), the school counselors looked at the root causes of their problem, and then they took systemic actions to improve the success rate of the 8th graders on the annual exam. Taking on the multiple roles of leader, advocate, manager of resources, and consultant, the counselors used the data to identify barriers and ultimately enact change where, when, and how it was needed. The three counselors at Riverdale Middle School were never left out of a school improvement conversation again!

Being able to use data in a meaningful way does not require that the school counselor needs to know how to physically pull data from the school system's database or to manipulate the system to aggregate and disaggregate the data. What the counselor does need to know is who to collaborate with to access the data. Knowing the power of data to help all students succeed, and knowing how to ask the right questions of the right people are the needed skills.

FROM PERCEPTION TO REALITY

Building your school counseling program around frequent analysis of critical data elements demonstrates a commitment to the issues and concerns that are important to all stakeholders, including legislators, school board members, teachers, parents, and both building and district level administrators. Data can tell a powerful story about the accomplishments of your students, especially when you use real numbers rather than relying on assumptions or perceptions. Concrete data such as enrollments in college prep courses, the graduation rate, retention rates, special education placements, attendance, grades, and standardized test scores are only a few examples. They can reveal a telling story of achievement patterns, equity issues, and the overall effectiveness of

Melissa Freeman, school counselor at Centennial High School in Roswell, Georgia, led a school wide initiative to improve ninth grade passing rates. Centennial was able to implement a plan that included a freshman summer camp and other, ongoing strategic activities. As a result of the involvement of all stakeholders, the school counseling department, administrators, teachers, staff, parents, business resources, and the students themselves, the results showed a significant decrease in the number of students who failed one or more 9th grade classes.

STEP FIVE: RESULTS

Intended Year of Graduation	Total Number of Students	Number of Students who Failed One or More Classes	Percentage of Students Failing One or More Classes
2010	502	165	32.87%
2011	515	142	27.78%

your school. A more complete list of critical and important data elements can be found in Appendix D.

Data gives your story a factual framework. No longer are we presenting perception; the descriptors in our school-based stories are rooted in reality. The analysis of data reveals every aspect of the conditions in our school and identifies those barriers that hinder student academic success.

CHALLENGE OR OPPORTUNITY: CARPE DIEM!

Using data to inform your thinking and the decisions that you make about your school counseling program will establish you as a school leader who is committed to school improvement.

FIGURE 2

Data can:

a. challenge attitudes and beliefs. Data tells the story to staff, faculty, parents, and students in a visual and in a nonjudgmental manner.

b. develop high expectations. The level of awareness and student expectations may differ among staff, parents, and students.

c. deliver facts that support on-going quality career and academic advising. Information is readily available to provide students and parents with current figures on scholarship dollars and financial aid information, as well as how to access the Internet for college and career advising.

d. alert us to enrollment patterns for rigorous academic courses. Aggregated and disaggregated data show the composition of our classrooms and course selection. Using data can influence course enrollment patterns and motivate and encourage students to accept the challenge.

e. impact the instructional program. School counselors can support the instructional program by assisting classroom teachers to use data to better understand the issues that impact achievement and behavior.

Strategies and activities that are intended to move these data from the baseline position to the identified goals are monitored throughout the implementation process. Benchmark data is collected along the way to monitor progress. When these indicators fall short, midstream course corrections can be put into place.

MEASURE AND MONITOR WHAT MATTERS

School counselors naturally observe much of what is happening in schools. Often the primary focus has been on monitoring and properly documenting the Carnegie units that students must accumulate for graduation at the high school level, or the basic skill proficiency attainment in reading and mathematics in K-8 assessments. These items still require careful scrutiny as schools and school systems continue to move toward a standards-based system of education. Most importantly, school counselors need to look, not only at the end results, but also at all of the data indicators that provide insight into how these results were achieved.

Select an example that reflects one of your school's improvement goals. Consider asking the following:

• What? How did the school counseling program contribute to a positive difference to the critical data elements selected by the school improvement team?

• When? Were these efforts ongoing or sporadic in their effort to meet the timeline established to reach school improvement goals?

• Who? Which students or groups of students are at highest risk?

• How? Which collaborative strategies will be implemented to realize your goal?

Accountability shows that all educators, especially school counselors, intentionally act to close the

The mission of Jackson County School District 9, in mutual partnership with the families and local community, is to prepare every student to be a self-directed, life long learner, a productive worker, and a responsible, contributing member of society.

Four schools—Shady Cove Elementary School, White City Elementary, White Mountain Middle School, and Eagle Point Middle School—with efforts led by counselors Susan Koury Barbara Reed and Michelle Vail, focused their efforts around a common goal, which was to decrease the number of disciplinary incidents for students who had been identified through the Student Study Team process by 20% by June 2009. Utilizing intentional strategies, discipline incidents were reduced in all three schools showing the power of teaming and collaboration among all stakeholders in a community wide effort! The data demonstrated how intervention and prevention strategies contribute to improving student achievement and helping every child succeed.

achievement gap (Dahir & Stone, 2007). Social justice and accountability go hand in hand. If administrators, faculty, and all other stakeholders truly believe that all children can learn and achieve, then aligning the purpose of school counseling with the goals of school improvement makes school counselors champions and collaborators who encourage high aspirations and create opportunities for students to realize their dreams. Accepting the challenge of accountability propels school counselors to remove barriers to learning and achievement, and raises the level of expectations for those students of whom little is expected. We do this by using data to monitor progress and measure the results of our efforts as contributing members of our school's educational community.

School counselors no longer view data as mysterious or overwhelming. We MEASURE and monitor what matters, that is, we pay close attention to the data that paints the picture of progress in our schools. Even when the results are confusing or even disappointing, we can use data to better understand what's going on and how, through collaboration and teaming, we can contribute to school success.

Data brings attention to opportunities for school-wide improvement through conversations and planning. Most importantly, data provides guidance for program development and implementation. School counselors who focus their school counseling program efforts on moving data in a positive direction demonstrate a strong commitment to sharing the responsibility and accountability for student outcomes.

REFERENCES

American School Counselor Association. (2003). *American school counselor association national model: A framework for school counseling programs.* Alexandria, VA: Author.

American School Counselor Association. (2005). *American school counselor association national model: A framework for school counseling programs.* 2nd edEd. Alexandria, VA: Author.

Collins, J. (2001). *Good to great.* New York: Harper Row.

Dahir, C., & Stone, C. (2003). *Accountability: A m.e.a.s.u.r.e. of the impact school counselors have on student achievement,* Professional School Counseling, 6, 214–221.

Dimmitt, C., Carey, J. & Hatch, T. (2007). *Evidence-based school counseling: Making a difference with evidence-based practices.* Thousand Oaks, CA: Corwin Press.

Education Trust (2001). *Achievement in America.* Retrieved July 25, 2009 from http://www2.edtrust.org/edtrust/

Education Trust National Center for Transformed School Counseling (2006). *Systemic school counseling: A blueprint for student success.* Module 1. Washington, D.C.: Author.

Hess, F. (2009). The new stupid. *Educational Leadership, 66.,* 12–17.

Johnson, C., Johnson, S. & Downs, L. (2006). *Building a results-based student support program.* Boston, MA: Houghton-Mifflin.

Light, D., Wexler, D., & Henize, J. (2004). *How practitioners interpret and link data to instruction: Research findings on New York City's school's implementation plan of the Grow Network.* Paper presented at the annual meeting of the American Educational Research association, San Diego, CA.

Martin, P.J. (2004). The school counseling role in closing achievement gap. Presentation delivered at teaching and learning academy, March 16, 2004, Memphis, TN: Author

McGonagill, G. (1992). *Overcoming barriers to educational restructuring: A call for system literacy.* ERIC, ED 357–512.

Peltzman, A. & Jerald, C. (2006). High standards and high graduation rates. The State Education Standard (December 2006), pp. 7–13 Retrieved June 30, 2009 from http://www.hsalliance.org/_downloads/NNCO/NASBESStanadrdDec06.pdf

Ronka, D. Lachat, MA, Slaughter, R, & Meltzer, J (2009). *Educational Leadership, 66,* 18–24.

Sagor (2005). *The action research guidebook: A four step process for educators and school teams.* Thousand Oaks, CA: Corwin Press

Secada, W. (2001). *From the director. Using data for educational decision making.* Newsletter of the Comprehensive Center Region VI, 6, 1–2.

Schmoker, M. (1999). *Results: The key to continuous school improvement (2nd edition).* Alexandria, VA: ASCD.

Schmoker, M. (2001) *The results field book: Practical strategies from improved schools.* Alexandria, VA: ASCD.

Schmoozer, M. (2006). *Results now.* Alexandria, VA: Association for Supervision and Curriculum Development.

Stone, C., & Turba, R. (1999). School counselors using technology for advocacy. *The Journal of Technology in Counseling, 1*(1). Available from http://jtc.colstate.edu/vol1_1/advocacy.htm

Weiss, J. (July 24, 2009). Race to the top. *Education Week On-Line,* p. 1.

Wiggins, G., & McTighe, J. (1998). *Understanding by design.* Alexandria, VA: ASCD.

CHAPTER 4

MEASURE: Six Steps to Improving Student Success

- Mission
- Elements
- Analyze
- Stakeholders-Unite
- Results
- Educate
- Systemic Change

MEASURE is a six-step accountability process that helps school counselors demonstrate how their programs affect critical data, those components of a school report card that are the backbone of the accountability. MEASURE stands for: Mission, Elements, Analyze, Stakeholders-Unite, Results, Educate.

MEASURE is a straightforward process designed to support the goals of the school leadership team and demonstrate that counselors are helping to drive critical data elements in a positive direction. MEASURE will help organize your efforts and show your results. MEASURE is a way of using information to target critical data elements, such as retention rates, test scores, and postsecondary-going rates, and using that data to develop specific strategies to connect school counseling to the agenda of your school.

Let's learn how to use the six steps by examining a very common goal for school districts, the improvement of postsecondary-going rates.

STEP ONE: MISSION

What Do I Need to Do?

Connect the design, implementation, and management of the school counseling program to the mission of the school and to the goals of the annual school improvement plan.

Student achievement and success in rigorous academics is at the heart of every school's mission statement. School counselors need to ask how every aspect of their program supports the mission of the school and contributes to student achievement. Preparing students to choose from a wide array of options after high school is part of every school district's mission for academic success and fulfilling the wishes of your school board.

STEP TWO: ELEMENT

What Do I Need to Do?

As a member of your school's leadership team, identify and examine the critical data elements in your school's improvement plan. School counselors play a pivotal role in this process as they work collectively with other stakeholders to focus on areas of opportunity for student success. Critical data elements can usually be found on your school's district or building report card. Chapter 4 provided you with a more detailed explanation of finding, analyzing, and using

---

MISSION
Connect your work to your school's mission in keeping with the ASCA or your state's comprehensive school counseling model.

Your school or department's mission statement is:
The mission of our school is to promote the conditions necessary for each student to succeed. Each student will complete the course work required to secure themselves a wide array of options after high school.

ELEMENT

What critical data element *are you trying to change? Examples include grades, test scores, attendance, promotion rates, graduation rates, postsecondary-going rate, enrollment in honors or AP courses, special education, discipline referral data, etc.*

What is the baseline *for the data element? Where do you hope to move it* (goal)*?*

Element: Postsecondary-going rate
Baseline: 50%
Goal: Increase the postsecondary-going rate this school year by 5%

---

critical data elements. School systems routinely collect and store academic and demographic data in a retrievable form. School counselors have ready access to that critical data which highlights opportunities to contribute to achievement, for example course enrollment patterns or attendance. Disaggregating data into separate elements in a variety of ways ensures that the system addresses access and equity issues. This approach to looking at data guarantees that no group of students is ignored.

Let us assume that the number of students in your school district continuing on to postsecondary educational institutions is not as high as it should be. Postsecondary institutions include all one-year technical institutes, two-year, and four-year colleges. Twenty-first century students need more than a high school diploma and less than a four-year college degree to become successful.

Postsecondary-going rates might be the critical data element to address in your school district. In our example, they have been holding steady around 50% for the last five years. Establish a baseline by identifying the data point that you will use for comparison to *measure* change. In this example, we will use 50% as the baseline for the postsecondary-going rate in our fictitious school district.

STEP THREE: ANALYZE

What Do I Need to Do?

Analyze the critical data elements to determine which areas pose problems. Analysis will expose the institutional or environmental barriers that are impeding student achievement, adversely influencing your data elements. Initially, school counselors can determine which elements to tackle, those the school counseling program wants to move in a positive direction, targeting specific goals. A quick look at data alone does not tell the whole story. It is important

---

ANALYZE

Analyze the data elements. You can use percentages, averages, raw scores, quartiles, or stanines. You can aggregate or disaggregate the data to better understand which students are succeeding. You can disaggregate by gender, race, ethnicity, socio-economic status, or in a multitude of ways to look at other student groupings.

The Baseline Data revealed: 50% of the class of 2009 attended a postsecondary institution.

Disaggregated Class of 2009 Demographics

Caucasian	49%
African American	31%
Hispanic	18%
Multi-racial	2%

Disaggregated postsecondary-going rate

Caucasian	80%
African American	21%
Hispanic	22%
Multi-racial	30%

Disaggregated data for students with formal career and educational plans

Caucasian	65%
African American	13%
Hispanic	22%
Multi-racial	25%

to disaggregate the critical data elements on which you are focusing, and to look at them in terms of gender, race/ethnicity, socioeconomic status, and perhaps by teacher to shed light on areas in need of attention.

In this example, these tables represent last year's graduating class. What do these tables tell you? What other information do you need to know? Which student groups are represented in the 50% who have accessed a postsecondary opportunity? Which students comprise the 50% who have not accessed this option?

As we said, you can disaggregate the data in a number of ways such as gender, ethnicity, socioeconomic status, home location (zip code), teacher or counselor assignments, course-taking patterns, feeder school patterns, etc. This information can be gathered by accessing the student information management system that your school uses.

AND THE DATA SAID...

In our example, when the data was disaggregated by ethnicity, it painted a picture of inequitable opportunity. As part of the school leadership team trying to improve critical statistics, what else do you need to know about this data? What are the key issues? How do you want this data to look next year and in subsequent years? How will the school counseling program contribute toward positive change in these critical data elements and connect the work of school counselors to better results for students?

When disaggregated even further, the data revealed (among other important things) that of the 50% of your students seeking postsecondary education, the majority or 34% came from one particular feeder middle school where all students were assigned to algebra classes in eighth grade and were supported with mentors and tutors to be successful.

The feeder middle school placed every student in algebra, a positive practice that could be replicated by the other feeder schools.

STEP FOUR: STAKEHOLDERS-UNITE

Identify stakeholders to involve in strategies to improve the data element.

What Do I Need to Do?

Identify stakeholders to include in the team to be involved in addressing positive change in the critical data elements. All concerned members of the internal and external school community should be included. Determine how to secure their commitment, and who will bring them together. If possible, use an existing school action committee. Accountability for school counselors is about collaborating with other stakeholders and avoiding tackling issues in isolation. Examples of stakeholders are:

Internal Community	External Community
Principal	Parent
Teacher	Business Representative
School Board Member	Faith-Based Group Representative

What Do I Need to Do?

Unite with stakeholders to develop, an action plan for improving critical data elements. Your collaborative plan should contain strategies, a timeline, and responsibilities in order to move the postsecondary-going rates to 55%. The table below gives a high school example of stakeholders and strategies that might be used. Similar tables can be created for middle and elementary school based on the target results from Step Three.

STAKEHOLDERS-UNITE TO DEVELOP STRATEGIES TO IMPACT THE DATA ELEMENT.

Beginning Date: September
Ending Date: June

Stakeholders	Strategies
School Counselors	• Implemented a career-awareness program for students in the school to help each other see the interrelatedness between postsecondary education and his or her future economic opportunities. • Advocated for a systemic change in course enrollment patterns to support more student access to higher level academics. • Used data and anecdotal information about student success in higher-level academics to change attitudes and beliefs about widening opportunities for higher-level academics.
Teachers	• Helped students research their career goals and project how their career paths fit with economic trends and the business climate (Social Studies). • Had students write essays for scholarships (English). • Integrated financial aid calculations into lessons (Math).
Administrators	• Provided professional development for the faculty to learn how to raise student aspirations. • Orchestrated collaboration with feeder schools to see how to replicate the practices that are proving successful in raising aspirations.
School Psychologists	• Provided additional group and individual counseling to high-risk students focused on motivation and problem solving.
School Social Workers	• Worked with parents and caretakers on teaching students the importance of attendance for school success.
Clerical Staff	• Monitored student progress in submitting applications for postsecondary admissions. • Organized group meetings between the counselors and the students who are not submitting information to postsecondary institutions in a timely manner.
School Clubs	• Invited community leaders to talk about career opportunities and the education and skills needed to be successful in the work environment. • Helped close the information gap by sponsoring awareness activities regarding postsecondary opportunities.
Parents	• Assisted in establishing a tutoring program. • Created a phone chain to call parents to remind them of important school events.
Volunteers	• Worked with individual students on the power of financial aid to impact their future.
Business Partners	• Assisted in establishing a mentoring program. • Provided site visits to their businesses. • Helped organize and participate in career fairs.
Community Agencies	• Assisted in establishing a mentoring program. • Ran evening and Saturday programs with school personnel for parents and students on raising aspirations, homework help, technology awareness, etc.
Colleges and Universities	• Hosted "College for a Day" programs for elementary and middle school students. • Offered diagnostic academic placement testing to tenth and eleventh graders. • Provided targeted interventions for underrepresented populations.

STEP FIVE: RESULTS

What Do I Need to Do?

Even if the targeted results were met, there is still reflection and refining to do. Did the results of everyone's efforts show that the interventions and strategies successfully moved the critical data elements in a positive direction? If so, reassess your efforts to develop your next steps toward continuous school improvement, including any changes in the school counseling program.

If the targeted results were not met, the next step would be to reanalyze and refocus the efforts to determine why the interventions were unsuccessful in moving the data in a positive direction. Identify the components of the effort that worked. Replicate what is working and develop new strategies for what did not work. Based on your analysis determine what changes need to be made to the school counseling program to keep the focus on student

success. We can't hold fast to programs and strategies that do not help our students become more successful learners. There is too much work and too little time to accomplish all that needs to happen for our students. A school counselor recently was lamenting, "What if I find that my conflict resolution program did not really impact the discipline rate?" (It did with a 54% decrease.) If the program had not made a difference, would we want to rethink investing so much time and energy? In other words, if the horse is dead, get off it! Most important is the conversation around which strategies were impactful and which weren't with the stakeholders and then adjusting the plan to focus on the goals the group hopes to accomplish. Sharing accountability is a process and it takes time to accomplish challenging goals and moving school improvement data in a positive direction.

It is always necessary to reanalyze to determine whether you met your targeted results. If the targeted

---

RESULTS

Restate your baseline data.
State where your data is now. Did you meet your goal?

Restate baseline data:
50% postsecondary-
going rate

Results (data now):
81% postsecondary-
going rate

Met Goal: Yes X No _____

Class of 2009

	2010 # of Seniors	2010% of Seniors	2010% to Post-secondary	2010 # to Post-secondary
Caucasian	150	59%	83%	123
African American	50	20%	30%	15
Hispanic	45	19%	27%	12
Multi-racial	4	2%	50%	2
	249		61%	152

Questions to consider as you examine results and revise your MEASURE:

Which strategies had a positive impact on the data?
All of them contributed. Especially helpful were the academic diagnostic assessments administered by our college partner.

Which strategies should be replaced, changed, added?
We need to reach out more to our community partners and find mentors and role models who will help us raise student aspirations.

Based on what you have learned, how will you revise Step Four "Stakeholders-Unite?"
Next year we are going to focus on the discrepancies in postsecondary-going rates among Caucasian, African Americans, and Hispanics, and examine course patterns beginning with 9th graders.

How did your MEASURE contribute to systemic change(s) in your school and/or in your community?
We are beginning to establish a postsecondary culture in our high school. Many of our teachers asked to establish an Alumni Day. They want to wear a shirt or hang a pennant from the college that they attended.

results were met, set new targets, add new strategies, and replicate what was successful. If the postsecondary rates increased by only 2% and thus fell short of the target, it will be necessary to refocus efforts to determine which strategies were successful and which need to be replaced or revised. Stakeholders will examine together what efforts worked well, and which strategies need to be modified, adjusted, or perhaps changed altogether. The next steps will be to revise the action plan for the following year and to continue to move the critical data elements in a positive direction.

Look at that high school profile now! Now 61% of our students are accessing postsecondary opportunities, even better than the goal of 55%. What did we learn from this process?

- Critical data element analyses helped us focus our efforts.
- District wide systemic change issues must begin in elementary school.
- Stakeholders across all levels were willing to share responsibility for moving critical data elements.
- Changes in data clearly demonstrated the intentional focus of the school counseling program on improving the postsecondary-going rate.
- Collaborative effort made the change happen.
- The school counselors' commitment as key players in school improvement was well established and acknowledged.

- Strategies delivered K through 12 positively moved this data forward.
- Measurable results showed how the school counseling program worked to increase the postsecondary-going rate through a system wide focused effort.

STEP SIX: EDUCATE

What Do I Need to Do?

Disseminate to internal and external stakeholders the changes in the targeted data elements that show the positive impact the school counseling program is having. Publicizing the results of an effective school counseling program is a vital step in the accountability process and key to garnering support for your program. This can be a time to celebrate success and recognize and applaud your partnerships. Through this education, stakeholders will have a deeper understanding about the contributions of the school counseling program focused on student achievement. School counselors will be seen as partners in school improvement and have demonstrated a willingness to be accountable for changing critical data elements. Because of these efforts, school counselors are viewed as essential to the mission of the school.

Educate others as to your efforts to improve the data. Develop a report card that shows how the work of the school counselor(s) is connected to the mission of the schools and to student success. Following is an example of a report card.

Presidential High School: MEASURE of Success

Principal: Elsie Davis

Enrollment: 2112

Counselors: Timothy Bishop, Gray Howell, Katie Handel, Amanda Riemer

Principal's Comments

Preparing students to choose from a wide array of options after high school is part of our district's mission of academic success for every student. Our counselors worked very hard this year to satisfy the school board's desire to improve the postsecondary-going rate for every student. They looked at the important data elements that contribute to improving our student's futures and used their leadership, advocacy, teaming, and collaboration skills to make a positive difference.

School Improvement Issues

Postsecondary-going rate is 50%. Underrepresented students do not transition to a wide variety of options after high school.

Stakeholders

Parents: Assisted in establishing a tutoring program; created a phone chain to call parents to remind them of important school events.

Community: Assisted in establishing a mentoring program; ran evening and Saturday programs with school personnel for parents and students on raising aspirations, homework help, and technology awareness.

Volunteers: Participated in training delivered by financial aid officers on the Free Application for Federal Student Aid (FAFSA); worked with individual students on the power of financial aid to impact their future.

Business Partners: Assisted in establishing a mentoring program. Provided site visits to their businesses. Helped organize and participate in career fairs.

Systemic Changes

Measurable results showed how the school counseling program worked to increase the postsecondary-going rate through a whole school and community effort to impact the instructional program.

Results

Comparative Changes in Postsecondary Rates

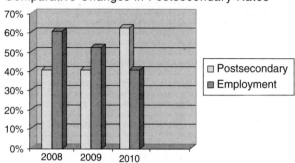

Percentages of Students by Ethnicity Accepted to Postsecondary Institutions

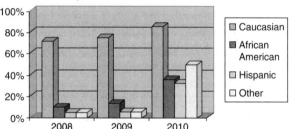

2010 DATA SUMMARY

CLASS of 2010	% of Seniors	% to Post-secondary
Caucasian	59%	83%
African American	20%	30%
Hispanic	19%	27%
Multi-racial	2%	50%
Total		61%

Faces Behind the Data

A parent approached her child's school counselor at the end of the graduation ceremony. "I didn't think my child's dream of going to college was going to happen this year," she said. "I am recently divorced and did not realize that financial aid would be available. Thank you for keeping after both us to fill out the FAFSA so that it wasn't too late to get some help."

NOTE: The **E**ducate step in MEASURE has been adapted with permission from the Student Personnel Accountability Report Card sponsored by the California Department of Education and Los Angeles County Office of Education.

SYSTEMIC CHANGE

Whenever you implement a MEASURE you will contribute to systemic change. Each MEASURE will in some way change a school, home, or community system to enhance student learning. Capture these systemic changes here and record them on your SPARC.

Dr. Dan Bullara, school counselor at Mt. View elementary, enthusiastically worked with his principal to make the systemic changes that ensured that 4th and 5th grade special needs students would succeed on the statewide reading test.

Jackson County School District #9 ~ Mt. View Elementary School
A MEASURE OF SUCCESS

Principal: Lisa Yamashita

School Counselor: Dr. Dan Bullara

Enrollment: 344

Framework for Success Members:

Administrators: Ginny Walker, Tiffany O'Donnell, Tina Mondale; **Teachers:** Judy Rosenzweig, Ken Welburn, Stephanie Pogue, Tim Rouhier; **ELL Coordinator:** Scott Townsend; **Administrative Support:** Shelly Ward, Claudia Spielbusch; **Special Education:** Barbara Seus, Terry Jacques, Bea Karcher

Principal's Comment

As a new administrator to Eagle Point School District, I have really enjoyed the commitment and energy these educators bring to work each day. I am truly excited about the work we have done in our Special Reading Class and, I know we will meet our goal of having all groups of students become better readers.
Lisa Yamashita, Principal, Mt. View Elementary School

School Counselor's Comment

This project was quite exciting, not only because I was able to directly work with the children on a daily basis, but because of the enthusiasm of the students and my fellow teachers for the project. Further, the support of our building principal made this project a reality. Finally, the stakeholders "behind the scene" are to be commended for their hard and dedicated work in supporting this program—to you and all the stakeholders, I thank you.
Dr. Dan Bullara, Counselor, Mt. View Elementary School

Critical Data Element (s)

To improve the average percent of students with special needs, or those identified at-risk, grade 4 and 5, who meet or exceed state standards on Reading Knowledge and Skills by increasing their averaged RIT score by 16.1 points by June 2009

Results

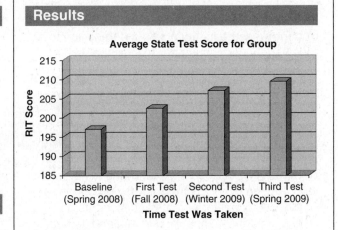

An overall increase of 11.6 RIT points for the group this year. This amounts to more than one and one-half years of growth for the 2008–2009 school year.

Systemic Changes

1. School-wide recognition of differentiated instructional strategies related to reading.
2. System-wide recognition for supporting students with special needs and those identified at risk.
3. Better collaboration between counseling, special education and general education in the services for students at-risk.

NOTE: The Educate step in MEASURE has been adapted with permission from the Student Personnel Accountability Report Card sponsored by the California Department of Education and Los Angeles County Office of Education.

When you take on the challenge of delivering a data-driven school counseling program, you become a systemic change agent, impacting policies and procedures that will widen opportunities and empower more students to be successful learners. If the system is working optimally, then a MEASURE would not be necessary; we can't drive data without changing systems. So, when you are gathering stakeholders and developing strategies, make certain you implement a MEASURE that intentionally tackles systemic barriers. Give yourself credit for impacting systems. Impacting systems means:

1. replicating successful programs and interventions,
2. identifying barriers that adversely effect students opportunities to be successful learners, and
3. developing strategies to:
   - change policies, practices, and procedures.
   - strengthen curriculum offerings.
   - maximize the instructional program.
   - enhance the school and classroom culture and climate.
   - provide student academic support systems (safety nets).
   - influence course enrollment patterns to widen access to rigorous academics.
   - involve parents and other critical stakeholders (internal and external to the school).
   - raise aspirations in students, parents, teachers, and the community
   - change attitudes and beliefs about students and their abilities to learn

---

THE STARFISH STORY

A man was walking along the beach. Hundreds of starfish had washed up on the shore. As he walked along he would pick one up and toss it back into the ocean. A passerby observed him and commented: "There are thousands. You can't possibly save them all!" The man smiled as he looked up and responded "Yes, but I can save this one!"
Source: unknown

The systemic change agent will not allow hundreds of starfish to swelter and die, saving just one. Rather, the systemic change agent will build a net to keep the starfish from beaching, study the situation to see what is causing the starfish to beach, or call in resources to help (Hines, 1999).

Additional MEASURE and Report card examples are presented in the next chapter.

Practice What You Have Learned

It is your turn to complete a MEASURE. Take one of the three scenarios below and fill in the blank MEASURE. For additional assistance, you can refer to the MEASURE examples in Chapter 5.

High School Counselors:
As part of the leadership team at your school you are trying to improve the preparation of your students for college by encouraging them to take an advanced placement course as part of a rigorous academic curriculum.

Middle School Counselors
As part of the leadership team at your school you are trying to help increase the number of students who are promoted from 8th grade to 9th grade. It has declined due to a new high stakes 8th grade test.

Elementary School Counselors
As part of the leadership team at your school you are trying to increase the number of 3rd grade students from below proficient in reading to proficient, as designated on your school's report card.

MEASURE is a simple yet thorough tool that focuses both on the tangible tasks and the critical relationships necessary to successfully implement a data-based decision making project for graduate students and practicing school counselors.

Dr. Tina Anctil, Assistant Professor, Counselor Education Portland State University

MEASURE

Mission, Element, Analyze, Stakeholders-Unite, Results, Educate
A Six-step Accountability Process for School Counselors

Name and Address of School:
Principal:
Name of Counselor(s) Leading the Initiative:
Enrollment:
School Demographics:

Caucasian/Non-Hispanic
African American
Hispanic
Asian/Pacific Islander
Native American
Multi-Racial
Free-Reduced Lunch
English as Second Language
Exceptional Student Education/Special Education

STEP ONE: MISSION

MISSION
Connect your work to your school's mission in keeping with the ASCA or your state's comprehensive school counseling model.

Your school or department's mission statement is:

STEP TWO: ELEMENT

ELEMENT
What critical data element *are you trying to impact? (Examples include grades, test scores, attendance, promotion rates, graduation rates, postsecondary-going rate, enrollment into honors or AP courses, special education, discipline referral data, etc.*
What is the baseline *for the data element? Where do you hope to move it* (goal)*?*

Element:
Baseline:
Goal:

STEP THREE: ANALYZE

ANALYZE THE DATA ELEMENT
You can use percentages, averages, raw scores, quartiles, or stanines. You can aggregate or disaggregate the data to better understand which students are meeting success. You can disaggregate by gender, race, ethnicity, socio-economic status, or a multitude of other ways to look at specific student groupings.

The Baseline Data revealed:

STEP FOUR: STAKEHOLDERS-UNITE

STAKEHOLDERS-UNITE TO DEVELOP STRATEGIES TO IMPACT THE DATA ELEMENT

Beginning Date:
Ending Date:

Stakeholders	Strategies
School Counselor(s)	■
Administrator(s)	■
Teachers	■
Students	■
Student Organizations (clubs, teams, etc.)	■
Parents	■
Parent Teacher Associations	■
School Psychologists	■
Social Workers	■
Community Agency Members	■
Faith-Based Organizations	■
Youth and Community Associations	■
Colleges and Universities	■
Classroom Teacher Assistants	■
Other Support Staff (front office, custodial, cafeteria, playground)	■
School Improvement Team	■
Resources (grants, technology, etc.)	■
	■
	■
	■

STEP FIVE: RESULTS

RESULTS:

Restate your baseline data.
State where your data is now. Did you meet your goal?

Restate baseline data: Results (data now):   Met Goal: Yes _____   No _____

Questions to Consider as you examine results and revise your MEASURE:

Which strategies had a positive impact on the data?

Which strategies should be replaced, changed, added?

Based on what you have learned, how will you revise Step Four "Stakeholders-Unite?"

How did your MEASURE contribute to systemic change(s) in your school and/or in your community?

STEP SIX: EDUCATE

Educate others as to your efforts to move data. Develop a report card that shows how the work of the school counselor(s) is connected to the mission of the schools and to student success. Below is an example of a report card.

(School Name) MEASURE OF SUCCESS

Principal:

Enrollment:

School Counselor(s):

Principal's Comment

Critical Data Element (s)

Systemic Changes

Stakeholders Involved

Counselor(s)

Administrator:

Teachers:

Parents:

Students:

Colleges and Universities:

Business Partners:

Results

Faces behind the Data

NOTE: The **E**ducate step in MEASURE has been adapted with permission from the Student Personnel Accountability Report Card sponsored by the California Department of Education and Los Angeles County Office of Education.

REFERENCES

Hines, P. (1999). *Transforming school counseling.* Annual conference of the Education Trust. Washington, DC.

CHAPTER 5

School Counselors Demonstrating Accountability

School counselors are challenged to demonstrate the effectiveness of their program in measurable terms. School counselors must collect and use data that support and link the school counseling program to students' academic success.

—The ASCA National Model, p. 59

Since 2003, thousands of hard-working, forward-thinking school counselors agreed to implement data-driven school counseling programs. Their admirable efforts resulted in the following 12 MEASUREs that represent elementary, middle, and high schools. Additionally, five school counseling leaders representing urban and suburban systems tell their story of engaging all school counselors in their systems in MEASURE and how that helped them promote the importance of school counseling.

Elementary Schools

Sheffield Elementary, Memphis, Tennessee

Sweet Apple Elementary, Roswell, Georgia

Westmoreland Elementary Westmoreland, Tennessee

Middle Schools

East Hampton Middle School, East Hampton, New York

Forest Park Middle School, Massachusetts

Westside Middle School, Memphis, Tennessee

High Schools

Dr. Freddie Thomas High School, Rochester

Lindenhurst High School, Lindenhurst, New York

High School for Media and Communications, New York, New York

John Overton High School, Nashville, Tennessee

LaVergne High School, LaVergne, Tennessee

West Haven High School, West Haven, Connecticut

School Systems

Connecticut Technical High School System

Rochester City School District, New York

Rutherford County Schools, Tennessee

Salem-Keizer Public Schools, Oregon

Springfield Public Schools, Massachusetts

This is such a huge accomplishment for the department for many reasons with 106 counseling staff, 99 completed MEASURES. It was amazing to see the shift from absolute fear and panic to excitement and enthusiasm for the process. So many light bulbs went on for so many staff. They will never approach their programs in the same way. MEASURE truly HAS transformed the way we approach our responsibilities and understand our role as school counselors. It has helped to punctuate, in a big way, the professional, in school counseling programs.

(Marilyn Rengert, Retired Program Associate, Counseling Department, Salem-Keizer Public Schools, Past President, Oregon School Counselor Association)

In the 12 MEASUREs that follow and in the School District Summaries you will see the changes in data that occurred in STEP 5 – Results! Every one of these school counselors, because of their commitment to social justice and their leadership influence, contributed to the academic success picture of their schools. Furthermore, they showed their contribution with hard data, not perceptions, not time-on-task, but real numbers that represent thousands of students who are better off as a result of their work!

As members of their schools' leadership teams, look at what these counselors have accomplished: decreasing high school suspension rates; increasing 7th grade passing rate; increasing elementary, middle and high school attendance rates; increasing ninth-grade promotion rates; increasing the four-year college going rate; increasing the passing rate for Algebra I; increasing elementary state test scores; and decreasing middle school discipline rates. The proof is here in the student outcomes.

These counselors will tell you that working in a focused way and connecting their efforts to the mission of the school have cast them in a more powerful, important light with the stakeholders of their schools.

As you read these MEASUREs, think about all the important changes these counselors were able to make on a macro, systemic level. Being an agent of systemic change is a powerful, heady role for a school counselor. When you make a systemic change, the number of students impacted increases dramatically. Think about the many public relations benefits that come from sharing the accountability report card. Educator Bob Tyra, of the Los Angeles County Office of Education, the creative force behind the design of the Student Personnel Accountability Report Card (SPARC), explains that SPARCs are widely distributed to realtors, businesses, the chamber of commerce, and the Parent Teacher Association. In other words, school counselors use their accountability report cards as important public relations tools for their programs, and also to educate their internal and external communities as to the contributions school counselors are making to student success. The SPARC template has been adapted with permission for these purposes as a complement to MEASURE.

The effects of quality school counseling are often hard to quantify. Yet, in this age of educational accountability, school counselors, like other educators, are being asked to provide evidence of the effects of their work on student achievement and success. In the past, gathering quantifiable evidence was often limited to time-on-task analyses. However, the issue at hand is no longer answering the question "What does a school counselor do?" The days of time-on-task analyses are over. Rather, MEASURE provides counselors a venue in which to ask the question, "How do I know that what I am doing is helping students?" It provides a forum for quality program evaluation and de-mystifies the accountability process for school counselors. MEASURE helps to guide counselors through the process of moving from intention to implementation—from implementation to impact.

(Kellie M. Hargis, Ed.D., Principal, Bellevue Middle School Metropolitan Nashville Public Schools and former Director of Guidance)

Our school counselor, Mrs. Benton, takes a leadership role and collaborates so that our students can succeed. As a result of her hard work with the leadership team we have a 77% reduction in office referrals. Mrs. Benton is an asset to Westside Middle School and Memphis City Schools.

(Willie C. Williams, Principal)

MEASURE

Mission, Element, Analyze, Stakeholders-Unite, Results, Educate
A Six-step Accountability Process for School Counselors

Name and Address of School:
Dr. Freddie Thomas High School
625 Scio Street, Rochester, New York 14605

Principal:
Sandra Jordan

Name of Counselor(s) Leading the Initiative:
Gail Leysath, Carsmon Binger, Hamid Charm, Angela Covich, Mary Parker-Gagliano, Diana Pino

Enrollment:
1,074

School Demographics:
Caucasian/Non-Hispanic: 8%
African American: 68%
Hispanic: 23%
Other: 1%
Free-Reduced Lunch: 98%
English as Second Language: 1%
Exceptional Student Education/Special Education: 18.1%

STEP ONE: MISSION

MISSION
Connect your work to your school's mission in keeping with the ASCA or your state's comprehensive school counseling model.

Your school or department's mission statement is:
Dr. Freddie Thomas High School's mission is to educate each student to the highest levels of academic performance and to foster each student's social and emotional development. We partner with families, caregivers, and the Rochester community to prepare students to meet or exceed standards, and to become lifelong learners, productive members of the workforce, and responsible, contributing citizens.

   The school counseling department's mission is to provide a comprehensive, developmentally age-appropriate and sequential school counseling program that is aligned with the New York State Learning Standards, the National ASCA standards, and state (NYSSCA) standards. As counselors, we focus on the needs, interests, and issues related to the stages of our students' growth through academic, career, and personal/social development. We work in partnership with students, staff, family, community members, and employers to prepare students to become effective learners, achieve success in school, live successful and rewarding lives, and develop into contributing members of society.

STEP TWO: ELEMENT

ELEMENT
What critical data element are you trying to impact? (Examples include grades; test scores; attendance; promotion rates; graduation rates; post-secondary-going rate; enrollment into honors or AP courses, special education; discipline referral data; etc.)
   What is the baseline *for the data element? Where do you hope to move it* (goal)?

Element: Long-Term and Short-Term Suspensions.
Baseline: Suspension rate in 2003–2004;
Long-term: 158; **Short-term:** 349.
Goal: Decrease suspensions by a minimum of 10% each year.

STEP THREE: ANALYZE

ANALYZE THE DATA ELEMENT
You can use percentages, averages, raw scores, quartiles, or stanines. You can aggregate or disaggregate the data to better understand which students are meeting success. You can disaggregate by gender, race, ethnicity, socio-economic status, or in a multitude of ways to look at student groupings.
See graphs.

The Baseline Data revealed:
Prior to 2003, Dr. Freddie Thomas High School was a school where student brawls were a daily occurrence and where the suspension rate was 51%.

STEP FOUR: STAKEHOLDERS-UNITE

STAKEHOLDERS-UNITE TO DEVELOP STATEGIES TO IMPACT THE DATA ELEMENT

Beginning Date: 2003–2004 school year
Ending Date: 2008–2009 school year

Stakeholders	Strategies
School Counselor(s)	• Collaborated with leadership team to change culture of the school. • Helped to break down the walls of isolation and, with the new leadership team, joined the school community in creating a culture of collaboration and cooperation. • Embraced commitment to the belief that all students can learn—"Titans to the Top" became the school motto. • Placed students in rigorous and engaging classes. • Embraced challenges with positive actions (i.e., group counseling). • "Adopted" seniors in an effort to increase graduation rate. • Implemented comprehensive school counseling programs with activities at each grade level.
Administrator(s)	• Instituted a new leadership team in the school that fostered a strong bond with school counselors and instructional staff to work collaboratively. • Completely reorganized and restructured the school to provide a safe environment for all who work and learn in the school. • Fostered and supported best practices. • Arranged for common planning time for teachers in order to break down traditional barriers for teacher interaction in secondary schools. • Engaged all members of the school community in a dramatic reform effort in school culture. • Continually asked "What's best for students?" and proceeded accordingly.
Teachers	• Engaged in co-teaching model. • Instituted "best practices" in instruction. • Teamed with counselors in "Adopt A Senior" program. • Participated in quality staff development programs. • Completed inquiry and problem-based training based on interests and strengths of students. • Developed rigorous and engaging classes for students.
Students	• Embraced the new learning environment. • Participated in student leadership development activities. • Improved attendance and achievement. • Improved behavior.
Parents	• Served on school-based planning teams. • Were involved in every step of the school transformation process.
Social Workers	• Teamed with counselors to provide intense support services to students.
Community Agency Members	• Recognized the changes that took place at Dr. Freddie Thomas and supported the school in its reform efforts. • Via Health • Hillside Work-Scholarship Connections

Stakeholders	Strategies
Faith-Based Organizations	• Participated in community building events at Dr. Freddie Thomas High School.
Colleges and Universities	• Provided mentors, tutors, and counselor practicum and internship graduate students.
Other Support Staff (front office, custodial, cafeteria, playground)	• Provided a safe environment for all who work and learn in the school.

STEP FIVE: RESULTS

RESULTS

Restate your baseline data.
State where your data is now. Did you meet your goal?

Restate baseline data: Results (data now):   Met Goal: Yes X No ____

	2003–2004	2004–2005	2005–2006	2006–2007	2007–2008	2008–2009
Short-term suspensions	349	381	473	200	224	160
Long-term suspensions	158	140	110	90	40	25

Questions to Consider as you examine results and revise your MEASURE:

Which strategies should be replaced, changed, added?

Continue to tell the stories of the change—retell the stories in an effort to bring new members into the community. As one teacher put it, "By celebrating what we overcame we realize how much more we can and must accomplish."

Based on what you have learned, how will you revise Step Four "Stakeholders-Unite?"

- Develop a school-wide Counseling Advisory Council with representatives from each instructional department, the business community, higher education, leadership, parents, students, counselors, and Central Office Director of Counseling.
- Increase parental involvement through counseling newsletters and press releases.
- Involve business partners in providing incentives to our students (i.e., school supplies, bookbags).

How did your MEASURE contribute to systemic change(s) in your school and/or in your community?

Through MEASURE, we focused on accountability and use of data to show the impact of counseling services. We published our results and, as a consequence, won the prestigious "National School Change Award" from the U.S. Education Department.

Dr. Freddie Thomas High School became a community of learners who work together to help both students and staff become a model for the country! In April 2009, Dr. Freddie Thomas High School won the prestigious "National School Change Award" from the U.S. Education Department. This award recognizes significant, sustained change. It is the only one of its kind and recognizes schools that have made significant and sustained improvements in student performance and school climate. The counselors at Dr. Freddie Thomas High School were an integral part of this change—and their principal, Sandra Jordan, and her leadership team support their counselors and recognize the value of their work as systems change agents and advocates for students.

STEP SIX: EDUCATE

Educate others as to your efforts to move data. Develop a report card that shows how the work of the school counselor(s) is connected to the mission of the schools and to student success. Below is an example of a report card.

Dr. Freddie Thomas High School MEASURE of Success

Principal: Sandra Jordan
School Counselor(s): Carsmon Binger, Hamid Charm, Angela Covich, Gail Leysath, Parker-Gagliano, and Diana Pino
Enrollment: 1,074

Principal's Comment

The role of the school counselor has impacted our school culture and directly impacts the reduction of suspensions. There are three areas of a student's life: home, school, and community. The school counselor is the link to all three areas. If you think of a triangle with the three areas, the school counselor is the link in the middle.

School Counselor(s)'s Comment

We became a cohesive counseling team as we worked diligently to institute a comprehensive school counseling program with classroom activities, group counseling, and collaborations with our community partnerships. As school counselors, we closely monitored each student's success and kept data on spreadsheets that tracked parental contacts, achievement data, credit checks, attendance data, and other supports.

Critical Data Element(s)

Dramatic decrease in short-term and long-term suspensions.

Systemic Changes

There was an increase in collaboration among the leadership team, counselors, teachers, and community representatives. The principal was instrumental in advancing the school counselors as being leaders and agents of school-wide systemic change.

Stakeholders Involved

Counselor(s): Involved all stakeholders in order to make MEASURE a school-wide initiative.
Administrator: Supported counselors' leadership in making MEASURE a school-wide initiative.
Teachers: Supported counselors in "Adopt A Senior" program, engaged in co-teaching model, embraced block scheduling model.
Parents: Changed attitudes and beliefs regarding the school, supported their children being in more rigorous classes, served on school-based planning teams and building committees.
Students: Improved attendance, behavior, and achievement.
Colleges and Universities: Provided mentors, tutors, and counselor practicum and internship graduate students.
Business Partners:
Provided support for school-wide events, provided mentors and tutors.

Results

The results were a decrease in short-term and long-term suspensions and a dramatic change in school climate and culture.

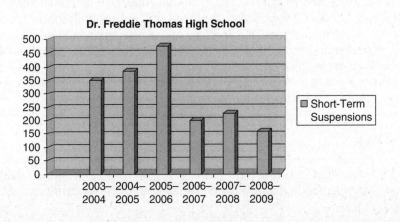

Dr. Freddie Thomas High School

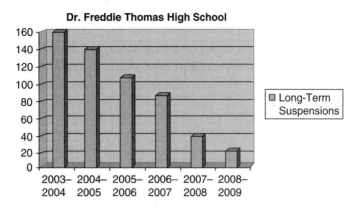

Dr. Freddie Thomas High School

| | Long-Term Suspensions |

Faces Behind the Data

- As one student said, "Thanks to our administrators, our new principal, our counselors and our teachers, Dr. Freddie Thomas High School has become a better high school and students have a better education and better opportunities in starting out their lives."
- Regarding the daily discussions of positive behavior, an 8th grader remarked, "We talk about how you're either going to be in the classroom, the cellblock or the cemetery".
- As one teacher said, "By celebrating what we overcame we realize how much more we can and must accomplish."

- As one staff member remarked, "The first five years were the easy changes. Now we need to work twice as hard to really make the important changes our children deserve."
- As a professor of education at a local college stated, "Today, Dr. Freddie Thomas High School is a place of respect, high expectations, pride, and scholarship. Behavioral and academic change has been no less than miraculous. The "miraculous" change has come about through knowledgeable and caring people whose work has resulted in strategic action, operational logic, focused instructional support, and unity in direction."

MEASURE

Mission, Element, Analyze, Stakeholders-Unite, Results, Educate
A Six-step Accountability Process for School Counselors

Name and Address of School:
East Hampton Middle School
76 Newtown Lane
East Hampton, NY 11937

Principal: Thomas Lamorgese, Ed.D.

Name of Counselor(s) Leading the Initiative: Bridget Anderson

Enrollment: 420

School Demographics:
Caucasian/Non-Hispanic: 58.6%
Hispanic: 31.4%
African American: 8.6%
Asian/Pacific Islander: 1.2%
Native American: 0.2%
Free-Reduced Lunch: 16.9%
English as Second Language: 4.5%
Exceptional Student Education/Special Education: 15.7%

STEP ONE: MISSION

MISSION
Connect your work to your school's mission in keeping with the ASCA or your state's comprehensive school counseling model.

Your school or department's mission statement is:
East Hampton Middle School is a teamed Middle School dedicated to providing a caring environment where all students are valued and their academic, social, and emotional growth is nurtured. We offer a challenging academic program and a rich array of electives. The after school program has an assortment of clubs, activities, and sports that will help young adolescents explore new interests and further develop established ones.

The EHUFSD Counseling Department is dedicated to providing a K-12 comprehensive program offering personalized developmental services that promote the social, emotional, and academic well-being of each student. Each school counselor is committed to assisting all students attain self-understanding and the skills and strategies necessary to become life-long learners, prepared to make informed decisions within the context of an ever-changing world.

STEP TWO: ELEMENT

ELEMENT
What critical data element are you trying to impact? (Examples include grades; test scores; attendance; promotion rates; graduation rates; post-secondary-going rate; enrollment into honors or AP courses, special education; discipline referral data; etc.
What is the baseline for the data element? Where do you hope to move it (goal)?

Element: 7th grade failure of two or more subjects.
Baseline: 129 students in 7th grade.
Goal: Reduce failure of 7th grade by 8%.

STEP THREE: ANALYZE

ANALYZE THE DATA ELEMENT

You can use percentages, averages, raw scores, quartiles, or stanines. You can aggregate or disaggregate the data to better understand which students are meeting success. You can disaggregate by gender, race, ethnicity, socio-economic status, or in a multitude of ways to look at student groupings.

The Baseline Data revealed:
The data was disaggregated by ethnicity each quarter:

	Students	1st quarter	2nd quarter	3rd quarter	Total number at-risk of failure of 2 or more subjects	% at-risk of failure of 2 or more subjects
Caucasian	75	2	2	5	9	12%
African-American	15	1	1	2	4	26.7%
Hispanic	39	2	0	2	4	10.3%

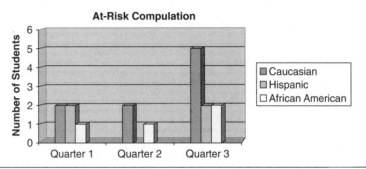

STEP FOUR: STAKEHOLDERS-UNITE

STAKEHOLDERS-UNITE TO DEVELOP STRATEGIES TO IMPACT THE DATA ELEMENT

Beginning Date: 11/6/09
Ending Date: 6/20/09

Stakeholders	Strategies
School Counselor(s)	• Attended team meetings; worked with teachers on motivators, organizational skills, and study skills. • Met with students individually to discuss their academics. • Made parent contacts weekly. • Conducted groups that specifically focused on areas of weakness or concern. • Created a peer mediation program. • Honored students with certificates for increasing academic progress.
Administrator(s)	• Met with students who were not succeeding. • Developed incentives.
Teachers	• Collaborated with counselors on providing student support, co-teaching study skills, organizational skills, etc.
Students	• Peer Mediators helped students understand how to get along with teachers.
Parents	• Attended workshop on motivating their child. • Signed an agreement with child.
Parent Teacher Associations	• Provided incentive certificates for students who improved from failing to passing.
School Psychologists	• Collaborated with counselors, teachers, and students.
Colleges and Universities	• Provided mentors from StonyBrook.
Classroom Teacher Assistants	• Provided on-going enthusiasm to help encourage students.
School Improvement Team	• Aligned goals of project with school improvement goals.

STEP FIVE: RESULTS

RESULTS

Restate your baseline data.
State where your data is now. Did you meet your goal?

Restate baseline data: Results (data now):   Met Goal: Yes X No ____

	Total # of students	1st quarter failures	2nd quarter failures	3rd quarter failures	4th quarter failures	Failures for the year
Caucasian	75	2	2	5	2	1
African-American	15	1	1	2	0	0
Hispanic	39	2	0	2	2	1
	129	5	3	9	4	2

*Out of 129 students in the 7th grade, 7% (9) were identified as "at-risk". Interventions reduced failures from 9 to 2.

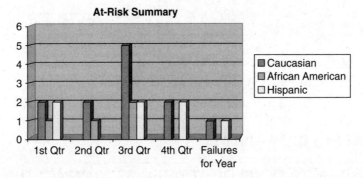

Questions to consider as you examine results and revise your MEASURE:

Which strategies had a positive impact on the data?
Establishing groups that specifically focused on areas of concern positively impacted the data. Groups included enhancing academic skills, exploring self-confidence, determining future plans, as well as examining different cultures.

Which strategies should be replaced, changed, added?
To help enhance communication between counselors and staff, counselors should be present during common times and other staff groupings involving student concerns.

Based on what you have learned, how will you revise Step Four, Stakeholders-Unite?
In the future, students that go from passing to failing should be recognized by our administration, as well as by their academic teachers.

How did your MEASURE contribute to systemic change(s) in your school and/or in your community?
It helped students become more positive about school and increased their confidence level by recognizing their accountability as a student.

STEP SIX: EDUCATE

Educate others as to your efforts to move data. Develop a report card that shows how the work of the school counselor(s) is connected to the mission of the schools and to student success. Below is an example of a report card.

East Hampton Middle School MEASURE of Success

Principal: Dr. Thomas Lamorgese
School Counselor(s): Bridget Anderson
Enrollment: 420

Principal's Comment

Ms. Anderson, although only three years in the profession, has a clear understanding of the role of the school. She has an excellent relationship with middle school students and has a strong interest in equity and excellence.

School Counselor(s)'s Comment

I feel it will be extremely interesting to follow this cohort and explore the comparison between this year and next year. Since this is my first MEASURE, I was a little unsure how everything would follow through, and now that I have this experience, I am excited to complete another MEASURE next year.

Critical Data Element(s)

Reduce failure rate by 8% in the 7th Grade for 2008–2009 school year.

Systemic Changes

Actions were established throughout the year that helped minimize student failures. Our psychologist implemented a child support team that united students, parents, and teachers to explore effective strategies to help students achieve.

Stakeholders Involved

Counselor: Conducted groups that specifically focused on areas of weakness or concern; honored students with certificates for increasing academic progress.
Administrator: Met with students who were not succeeding; developed incentives.
Teachers: Supported school counselor by making referrals and increasing communication among support staff.
Parents: Attended school meetings and conferences that focused on helping their child succeed.
Students: Learned effective study habits and motivational tools to keep them from failing.

Results

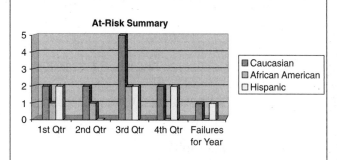

At-Risk Summary

Faces Behind the Data

It was rewarding to see the students stop by my office each week to check on their academic progress. One of the 7th graders told his friend that he learned how to change the behaviors that hindered his ability to achieve. The student said that the counseling curriculum really helped him to learn good study skills and effective study habits. He was excited to tell me that the guidance class really motivated him to want to pass all of his subjects! He said how much he appreciated that I was there for him and that I had helped him to do better in school.

MEASURE

Mission, Element, Analyze, Stakeholders-Unite, Results, Educate
A Six-step Accountability Process for School Counselors

Name and Address of School:
Forest Park Middle School
46 Oakland Street
Springfield, MA 01108

Principal:
Mrs. Bonnie Osgood

Name of Counselor(s) Leading the Initiative: Margaret Wynne, School Adjustment Counselor/ Guidance Chair; Raul Gonzalez, Kara Adams and Guidance Counselors; and Graduate Counseling Interns: Daniel Connors and Monica Bellucci.

Enrollment: 890

School Demographics:
Caucasian/Non-Hispanic: 15.4%
African American: 27.3%
Hispanic: 53.4%
Asian/Pacific Islander: 0.1%
Native American: 0.2%
Multi-Racial: 3.5%
Free-Reduced Lunch: 80.6%
English as Second Language: 27.7%
Exceptional Student Education/Special Education: 25.9%

STEP ONE: MISSION

MISSION
Connect your work to your school's mission in keeping with the ASCA or your state's comprehensive school counseling model.

Your school or department's mission statement is:
Just as a triangle has three sides, we believe that our tradition of academic excellence is due to our three-way collaboration of staff, students and community. At Forest Park Middle School, our mission is to maintain a safe environment in which our students are respectfully treated to data-driven, rigorous lessons. We believe that when all three sides of the academic triangle support each other, all of our graduates will be successful in high school, college and beyond.

STEP TWO: ELEMENT

ELEMENT
What critical data element are you trying to impact? (Examples include grades; test scores; attendance; promotion rates; graduation rates; post-secondary-going rate; enrollment into honors or AP courses, special education; discipline referral data; etc.
What is the baseline for the data element? Where do you hope to move it (goal)?

Element: Attendance rates.
Baseline: Aggregate attendance was 90.8%.
Goal: Aggregate attendance will increase to 92%.

STEP THREE: ANALYZE

ANALYZE THE DATA ELEMENT

You can use percentages, averages, raw scores, quartiles, or stanines. You can aggregate or disaggregate the data to better understand which students are meeting success. You can disaggregate by gender, race, ethnicity, socio-economic status or in a multitude of ways to look at student groupings.

The Baseline Data revealed:
Limited English, Hispanic, and Special Education have the lowest scores for attendance. The goal will be to raise our aggregate attendance rate to 92%.

Attendance Rates

Aggregate	Limited English	Special Education	Low Income	African American	Asian/ Pacific Islander	Hispanic	White
90.8%	89.4%	89.5%	90.3%	90.7%	95.4%	89.5%	91.1%

STEP FOUR: STAKEHOLDERS-UNITE

STAKEHOLDERS-UNITE TO DEVELOP STRATEGIES AND TO IMPACT THE DATA ELEMENT

Beginning Date: September 2008
Ending Date: June 2009

Stakeholders	Strategies
School Counselor(s)	• Assigned graduate interns to run attendance lunch groups. • Facilitated lunch groups for students with excessive absences/tardies. • Communicated with teachers and parents to address attendance issues. • Used reward program for improved attendance. • Went on home visits with the Attendance Officer. • Developed an individual plan for students with chronic attendance issues. • Middle School Transition Program-assigned 20 8th grade Hispanic students who were repeaters with excessive absences a weekly meeting during and after school through June 2009. • Provided quarterly parent workshops supporting attendance for parents whose children were in the ELL Program as a means to engage families in the school.
Administrator(s)	• Provided incentives for perfect attendance. • Met with Attendance Officer daily. • Attended weekly meetings with Guidance Department. • Implemented a call home program to identified risk group each week.
Teachers	• Requested parent-teacher conferences. • Participated in an action plan to support student attendance. • Participated in evening parent workshops.
Students	• Participated in developing an action plan to support daily attendance. • Participated in student lunch groups.
Parents	• Participated in workshops to support their child's attendance. • Participated in conferences with the counselor, teacher, and Attendance Officer.

Stakeholders	Strategies
Community Agency Members	• Participated in advisory meetings; collaborated with FPMS on referrals and interventions • Department of Child and Family Services • Child Guidance • Valley Psychiatric • Key Program • Juvenile Justice System Department of Transitional Assistance

Colleges and Universities	• Provided Graduate Interns:
	  –Springfield College
	  –Cambridge College

Parent Liason	• Provided funding for evening workshops; contacted parents and linked with community supports; met with counselors on a weekly basis; participated in home visits with the Attendance Officer; provided incentives for attendance.
Attendance	• Met with counselors on a daily basis to share attendance information and identify students at-risk; File School CHINS.
Resources (grants, technology, etc.)	• Provided incentives for attendance. • Friendly's Corporation • Burger King Corporation

STEP FIVE: RESULTS

RESULTS

Restate your baseline data.
State where your data is now. Did you meet your goal?

Restate baseline data: Results (data now):   Met Goal: Yes X No ____

Baseline	MP1	MP2	MP3	MP4
90.8%	95.65%	96.5%	93.4%	95.4%

Questions to Consider as you examine results and revise your MEASURE:

Which strategies had a positive impact on the data?
• Increased communication by meeting as a team weekly to discuss attendance issues.
• Increased involvement of the Parent Facilitator engaging with parents and students concerning the tracking of their attendance contracts.
• Daily lunch groups (3) with students at-risk to support their ongoing attendance at school each day.
• Parent workshops sponsored by the Parent Facilitator in which the School Adjustment Counselor presented on supporting your child attending school daily.

Based on what you have learned, how will you revise Step Four "Stakeholders-Unite?"
We learned how invaluable the Stakeholders were in supporting our attendance initiative. Our success could not have been as successful if we had not used a wide, diverse network.

How did your MEASURE contribute to systemic change(s) in your school and/or in your community?
Our MEASURE assisted us in having a more focused effort in working for change in our attendance. We were able to engage more parents in supporting our efforts.

STEP SIX: EDUCATE

Educate others as to your efforts to move data. Develop a report card that shows how the work of the school counselor(s) is connected to the mission of the schools and to student success. Below is an example of a report card.

Forest Park Middle School MEASURE OF SUCCESS

Principal: Bonnie Osgood
School Counselor(s): Margaret Wynne, Kara Admans, and Raul Gonzalez
Enrollment: 890

Principal's Comment

The Forest Park Middle School Attendance Initiative had been instrumental to a successful 2008–2009 school year. As we often say, "We cannot teach the children if they are not in school." A 4.6% increase in attendance equates to an additional 41 students in class, which can only lead to higher student achievement.

School Counselor(s)'s Comment

Our department has analyzed the data on the results of interventions related to increasing student attendance and achievement and created strategies for expanding our efforts with our stakeholders. As a result, there were significant changes in attendance, attitudes, behaviors, and overall commitment to their education.

Critical Data Element(s)

Element: Attendance rates.
Baseline: Aggregate attendance was 90.8%.
Goal: Aggregate attendance will meet a 92% attendance rate.

Systemic Changes

The implementation of this initiative impacted our department in a significant way. We had a marked increase in collaboration with parents, community providers, faculty, and other support staff in the school and district. We realized that we had various untapped resources that became pivotal to the success of our work.

Stakeholders Involved

Counselor(s): Communicated with teachers and parents to address attendance issues.
Administrator(s): Attended weekly meetings with Guidance Department.

Teachers: Participated in an action plan to support student attendance.
Parents: Participated in workshops to support their child's attendance.
Students: Participated in developing an action plan to support daily attendance.
Colleges and Universities: Provided graduate interns.
Business Partners: Provided incentives for attendance.

Results

Baseline	MP1	MP2	MP3	MP4
90.8%	95.65%	96.5%	93.4%	95.4%

Goal: 92%
Increase in attendance is 4.6%

Faces Behind the Data

This initiative made a significant impact on some students. It was not uncommon for a student who historically was truant to inform us of where they were in their attendance contract. A brother and sister who for three years rarely came to school (and if they did they were consistently late) would seek us out to let us know they were in school once we contracted with them and began tracking their attendance. They also monitored their own progress to make sure we knew they had earned their incentives. Many of our students began tracking and informing us of their progress proudly! Our daily lunch groups not only supported our attendance initiative, but also provided some of these students with positive social opportunities and an adult that they knew was counting on seeing them.

MEASURE

Mission, Element, Analyze, Stakeholders-Unite, Results, Educate
A Six-step Accountability Process for School Counselors

Name and Address of School:
High School for Media and Communications
George Washington Educational Campus
549 Audubon Avenue
New York, NY 10040

Principal:
Ms. Ronni Michelen

Assistant Principal:
Dr. JoAnn Sainz, Assistant Principal for Pupil Personnel Services
Mr. Dyanand Sugrim, Science/Security

Name of Counselor(s) Leading the Initiative:
Joan Apellaniz, Bilingual School Counselor

Attendance Team Members:
Bienvenida Galvez, Attendance Teacher
Dersa Gonzalez, Parent Coordinator
Elba Perez, Family Assistant
Jocelyn Bula, School Aide
Mariluz Mercado, School Aide
Linda Carbonell, School Aide
Mercedes Rodriguez, Secretary

Enrollment: 664

School Demographics:
African American: 5%
Hispanic: 93%
Asian/Pacific Islander: 2%
English language learner: 21%
Special education: 12%
Title 1: 83%

STEP ONE: MISSION

MISSION
Connect your work to your school's mission in keeping with the ASCA or your state's comprehensive school counseling model.

Your school or department's mission statement is:
The mission of the High School for Media and Communications, a small learning community, is to inspire our students to think critically and communicate clearly; to master a rigorous, well-rounded, academic curriculum with a basis in media and communications; to value their own heritage while also developing a global perspective on cultural, social, and environmental issues; to appreciate creative expression; and to incorporate integrity, responsibility, honesty, loyalty, and diligence in their professional and personal lives. The community, which will include students, parents, teachers, administrators, the public and private sectors, local community members, colleges, and universities, will operate under a covenant that will be synergistic and harmonious.

STEP TWO: ELEMENT

ELEMENT
What critical data element are you trying to impact? (Examples include grades; test scores; attendance; promotion rates; graduation rates; post-secondary-going rate; enrollment into honors or AP courses, special education; discipline referral data; etc.
What is the baseline for the data element? Where do you hope to move it (goal)?

Element: Attendance.
Baseline: 85.6% in 2006–2007 and 83.6% in 2007–2008.
Goal: Improve attendance rate by 1%.

STEP THREE: ANALYZE

ANALYZE THE DATA ELEMENT
You can use percentages, averages, raw scores, quartiles, or stanines. You can aggregate or disaggregate the data to better understand which students are meeting success. You can disaggregate by gender, race, ethnicity, socio-economic status, or in a multitude of ways to look at student groupings.

The Baseline Data revealed:

Year	Attendance Rate
2006–2007	85.6%
2007–2008	83.6%

STEP FOUR: STAKEHOLDERS-UNITE

STAKEHOLDERS-UNITE TO DEVELOP STRATEGIES TO IMPACT THE DATA ELEMENT
Beginning Date: September 2008
Ending Date: June 2009

Stakeholders	Strategies
School Counselor(s)	• Met with students regarding attendance issues. • Conducted planning interviews. • Participated in the school's attendance committee meetings. • Met with students and parents on an on-going basis. • Utilized data management, record keeping and attendance systems. • Conducted one on one counseling. • Made presentations to teachers, students, and parents. • Visited classes and stressed the importance of attendance and its impact on academics.
Administrator(s)	• Ensured the school had a functioning attendance program and monitored its effectiveness. • Ensured the school complied with all regulations regarding attendance. • Established an attendance committee and held regular attendance team meetings. • Set goals and monitored attendance trends.

Stakeholders	Strategies
Attendance Coordinator	• Supervised day-to-day activities of the members of the attendance team. • Made sure processes were in place for daily tracking of attendance. • Followed-up on all open long-term absentees. • Developed incentive programs for the school. • Reviewed all attendance data. • Met with attendance team member and the principal to discuss attendance issues. • Ensured all cases of educational neglect were reported and followed-up on. • Met with the attendance teacher to investigate and find resolution to any open long-term absentees.
Attendance Teacher	• Monitored student attendance and followed-up on cases of non-attendance. • Made home visits and assisted in resolving cases that could not be resolved on the school level. • Provided resources to schools on attendance matters. • Met with students regarding attendance. • Reported cases of educational neglect. • Participated in school attendance committee meetings. • Conducted all "address unknown" investigations. • Assisted in training school staff on attendance procedures. • Conducted the initial investigation on all open long-term absentees. • Updated attendance system. • Made initial phone calls. • Tracked any changes (address, phone, etc.).
Family Assistant	• Distributed, collected, and corrected daily attendance sheets. • Contacted parents. • Utilized attendance system to input and edit any changes • Filed data and made follow-up calls as needed. • Acted as contact person for late students.
School Aide	• Made initial phone calls. • Sent letters. • Monitored attendance data. • Contacted parents. • Interpreted. • Assisted with motivational events.
Parent Coordinator	• Attended team meetings. • Met with parents. • Planned special events. • Completed Face-to-Face letters. • Assisted in awards presentations. • Developed charts for data presentation. • Attended relevant workshops. • Convened daily with administrators and staff. • Contacted community-based organizations. • Organized cultural events. • Referred special needs students and parents to basic clinic.

STEP FIVE: RESULTS

RESULTS

Restate your baseline data.
State where your data is now. Did you meet your goal?

Restate baseline data: Results (data now):   Met Goal: Yes <u>X</u> No _____

By June 2009, school attendance will increase by 1%.

Year	Attendance Rate
2006–2007	85.6%
2007–2008	83.6%
2008–2009	85%

Questions to Consider as you examine results and revise your MEASURE:

Which strategies had a positive impact on the data?
The involvement of more stakeholders had a positive impact on the data.

Which strategies should be replaced, changed, added?
High school attendance is an on-going problem in this large urban school. In order to help improve student attendance, school counselors must work closely with our Attendance Committee, which will assist in contacting homes of students failing due to absence.

Based on what you have learned, how will you revise Step Four "Stakeholders-Unite?"
We will continue to work with the Attendance Committee in the High School for Media and Communications and do our best to involve everyone i.e., parents, guardians, teachers, community members, and the students themselves and ultimately continue to improve the attendance rate.

How did your MEASURE contribute to systemic change(s) in your school and/or in your community?
Student attendance is increasing because of the intervention of our stakeholders. We implemented data-driven decision-making to monitor the data frequently.

STEP SIX: EDUCATE

Educate others as to your efforts to move data. Develop a report card that shows how the work of the school counselor(s) is connected to the mission of the schools and to student success. Below is an example of a report card.

High School for Media and Communications George Washington Educational Campus
MEASURE of Success

Principal: Ronni Michelen
School Counselor(s): Joan Apellaniz, Mercedes Valdivia, Charity Halsdorf
Enrollment: 664

Principal's Comment

The High School for Media and Communications counselors worked very hard this year to improve students' attendance. Ms. Apellaniz took a leadership role by looking at attendance data carefully, because attendance is critical to our graduation rate and improving our students' futures. She used her leadership, advocacy, teaming, and collaboration skills to make a positive difference.

School Counselor(s)'s Comment

Success in education and attendance go hand-in-hand and it is our collective duty to develop creative, literate, self-disciplined, and responsible individuals. The collaboration of the school counselors with key stakeholders who are committed to improving student results contributed to raising the attendance rate.

Critical Data Element(s)

Improve the Attendance by 1%.

Systemic Changes

- The counselor initiated data-driven decision-making.
- Our actions are more student/parent-centered.
- The collaboration of counselor and the stakeholders improved school climate by creating an Attendance Committee.

Stakeholders Involved

Counselor(s): Studied data and implemented strategies to reduce the attendance rate.
Administrator: Supported the counselor and the key stakeholders to implement strategies to improve attendance rates. Demonstrated appreciation for the spirit of collaboration involving the counselor and stakeholders.
Teachers: Monitored student attendance and followed up on cases of non-attendance.
Parent Coordinator: Worked with the attendance team to contact parents.

Results

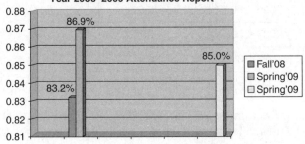

Total Average: Statistics for the School Year 2008–2009 Attendance Report

Fall'08
Spring'09
Spring'09

Faces Behind the Data

A 10th grade student arrived at our school this year with a history of truancy and family issues. Little by little, I was able to explain to her the importance of getting an education, and that it is a way out from the situation that made her unhappy. Although she was on academic probation at the beginning of the year, with the involvement of her parent and support from her counselor, her attendance situation began to improve. I was able to help her get an internship at Columbia University for the summer, which became a motivator for her to finish this school year with 15 absences, which was a huge improvement over last year. She is well on her way to turning the corner, coming to school every day, passing her classes, and graduating on time.

MEASURE

Mission, Element, Analyze, Stakeholders-Unite, Results, Educate
A Six-step Accountability Process for School Counselors

Name and Address of School:
La Vergne High School
250 Wolverine Trail
La Vergne, TN 37086

Principal:
Mr. Melvin Daniels

Name of Counselor(s) Leading the Initiative:
Scherrie Anderson, Stacie Frazier, and Steven Lay

Enrollment:
2016

School Demographics:
Caucasian/Non-Hispanic: 51.4%
African American: 30.8%
Hispanic: 13.0%
Asian: 4.8%
Pacific Islander: 0.1%
Native American: 0.1%
Free-Reduced Lunch: 40.5%
English as Second Language: 13.7%
Special Education: 10.6%

STEP ONE: MISSION

MISSION
Connect your work to your school's mission in keeping with the ASCA or your state's comprehensive school counseling model.

Your school or department's mission statement is:
The mission of Rutherford County School Counselors is to serve as student advocates, providing a comprehensive school counseling program that facilitates the academic, career, and personal/social development of all students in an academic environment.

STEP TWO: ELEMENT

ELEMENT
What critical data element are you trying to impact? (Examples include grades; test scores; attendance; promotion rates; graduation rates; post-secondary-going rate; enrollment into honors or AP courses, special education; discipline referral data; etc.
What is the baseline for the data element? Where do you hope to move it (goal)?

Element: 9th grade promotion rate.
Baseline: 70 9th graders identified as at-risk of failure.
Goal: Increase ninth grade promotion rate.

STEP THREE: ANALYZE

ANALYZE THE DATA ELEMENT
You can use percentages, averages, raw scores, quartiles, or stanines. You can aggregate or disaggregate the data to better understand which students are meeting success. You can disaggregate by gender, race, ethnicity, socio-economic status, or in a multitude of ways to look at student groupings.

The Baseline Data revealed:
Different subgroups are passing courses at different success rates. For example, more males are failing at a higher rate than females.

STEP FOUR: STAKEHOLDERS-UNITE

STAKEHOLDERS-UNITE TO DEVELOP STRATEGIES TO IMPACT THE DATA ELEMENT

Beginning Date: September 2008
Ending Date: June 2009

Stakeholders	Strategies
School Counselor(s)	• Met individually with at-risk students. • Contacted parent(s) or guardian(s). • Helped students learn to take responsibility for their actions. • Informed other counselors of the plan. • Reviewed report cards each six-week period for progress. • Organized group sessions regarding success in high school. • Referred students to the Graduation Coach for extra help.
Administrator(s)	• Provided support for targeted students after report cards were distributed. • Attended parent/teacher conferences as necessary. • Provided incentives for successful completion of work. • Identified students with special needs (IEP, 504, etc).
Graduation Coach	• Met with at-risk students to discuss the importance of passing classes and attendance toward graduation. • Explored outside opportunities for students to earn academic credit. • Communicated with middle schools to identify potentially at-risk students. • Used test scores to predict student success in classes. • Ran reports to check absences, dropouts, transfers and truancy.
Teachers	• Provided grade/credit recovery opportunities for a grade between 50–69 and no 0s. • Offered tutoring as needed. • Received detailed information to prepare students for Gateways and End-of-Course exams. • Consulted with counselors regarding student behavior. • Met with parents to discuss students and their needs. • Contacted parents via phone or email to keep them up to date on the student's progress. • Identified students with special needs (IEP, 504, etc).
Students	• Participated in small groups. • Met with counselor on an individual basis. • Participated in grade/credit recovery as needed.
Parents	• Attended IEPs. • Communicated with teachers and counselors. • Took an active role in the students' education. • Came to open houses/orientation. • Scheduled parent/teacher conferences as needed.

Stakeholders	Strategies
School Psychologists	• Attended IEPs. • Evaluated students for possible learning disabilities. • Counseled students as needed.
Community Agency Members	• Offered outside tutoring services as available.
Attendance Officer	• Sent letters home after five unexcused absences. • Contacted parents after ten unexcused absences.

STEP FIVE: RESULTS

RESULTS

Restate your baseline data.
State where your data is now. Did you meet your goal?

Restate baseline data: Results (data now):   Met Goal: Yes X No _____

September 2008: 70 9th Graders identified as at-risk of failure based on 1st six weeks grading period

2008–09	1st Six Weeks	2nd Six Weeks	3rd Six Weeks	4th Six Weeks	5th Six Weeks	6th Six Weeks	Final Grade	Promotion to 10th Grade
9th Graders	70	37	45	36	36	29	36	48

Questions to Consider as you examine results and revise your MEASURE:

Which strategies had a positive impact on the data?
Interventions by the Graduation Coach; meeting individually with the counselors; grade/credit recovery opportunities; and weekly parent conferences.

Which strategies should be replaced, changed, added?
More tutoring opportunities; at-risk students actually participating in grade/credit recovery; lack of parental involvement; lack of student motivation.

Based on what you have learned, how will you revise Step Four "Stakeholders-Unite"?
We will continue to work with teachers to strongly recommend grade/credit recovery to those students who are deemed at-risk; continue working with Graduation Coach to increase recovery opportunities; work to attain more parent involvement; work with administration to increase incentives for successful students.

How did your MEASURE contribute to systemic change(s) in your school and/or in your community?
Helping to determine which students were at-risk and providing them the available opportunities for acquiring recovery credit.

STEP SIX: EDUCATE

Educate others as to your efforts to move data. Develop a report card that shows how the work of the school counselor(s) is connected to the mission of the schools and to student success. Below is an example of a report card.

La Vergne High School MEASURE of Success

Asst. Principal: Dr. Wayne Coward
School Counselor(s): Scherrie Anderson, Stacie Frazier, and Steven Lay
Enrollment: 2016

Assistant Principal's Comment

The implementation of this program produced dramatic results. The initial goal was to reduce the number of 9th grade students who received two or more Fs on their report card by 10%. There were 70 freshmen initially identified. This number dropped to 37 receiving two or more Fs by the 2nd six weeks. The numbers remained steady throughout the year. In the end, 48, or 69%, of the original 70 students were promoted to the 10th grade. The results show the benefits that they received through the collaborative efforts of school counselors, the graduation coach, teachers, and administrators. Meeting the needs of at-risk students entering high school is the key for them to achieve academic success.

School Counselor(s)'s Comment

We decided to continue our focus on identifying 9th graders who were at-risk of failure. We identified these students based on the first grading period of their 9th grade year. We tracked them through subsequent six-week periods to identify and address needs.

Systemic Changes

Provided new interventions to the success rate of students who are considered at-risk.

Stakeholders Involved

Counselor(s): Met individually with at-risk students; contacted parent(s) or guardian(s); helped students learn to take responsibility for their actions; reviewed report cards each six week period for progress; organized group sessions regarding success in high school.
Graduation Coach: Met with at-risk students on a regular basis to provide support; implemented programs to help students with grade and credit recovery opportunities.
Administrator: Supported targeted students after report cards were distributed; attended parent/teacher conferences as necessary.
Teachers: Offered grade/credit recovery opportunities; provided tutoring; consulted with counselors regarding student behavior.

Parents: Communicated with teachers and counselors; took an active role in the students' education.
Students: Participated in small groups; met with counselors on an individual basis; participated in grade/credit recovery as needed.

Critical Data Element

The School Counselors identified the ninth grade promotion rate to ensure students are academically prepared for post-secondary education as the critical data element.

Results

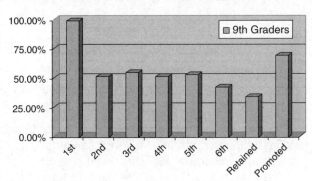

69% of the original 70 9th graders identified as at-risk were promoted to the 10th grade.

Faces Behind the Data

In an effort to improve both promotion and graduation rates, we chose to focus on our struggling 9th graders. Two of our students were freshman for the second time and in danger of spending a 3rd year as 9th graders. They did not realize what was available to them until we provided them with options through the school. The students connected with our graduation coach who provided them with ways to recover credits. Together with their teachers, we ensured regular parent contact. The students told us that because we provided them with the supports to achieve success, they were able to step up and do what was needed. A happy ending—both of these students recovered enough credits to be promoted to juniors for their third year of high school.

MEASURE

**Mission, Element, Analyze, Stakeholders-Unite, Results, Educate
A Six-step Accountability Process for School Counselors**

Name and Address of School:
Lindenhurst High School
300 Charles Street
Lindenhurst, NY 11757

Principal:
Daniel E. Giordano

Name of Counselor(s) Leading the Initiative:
Barbara A. Donnellan, Ed.D.

Enrollment:
2395

School Demographics:
Caucasian/Non-Hispanic: 85.4%
African American: 2.0%
Hispanic: 10.6%
Asian/Pacific Islander: 1.9%
Native American: <1%
Free-Reduced Lunch: 14.3%
English as Second Language: 2.3%
Exceptional Student Education/Special Education: 9.9%

STEP ONE: MISSION

MISSION
Connect your work to your school's mission in keeping with the ASCA or your state's comprehensive school counseling model.

Your school or department's mission is:
It is the mission of the Lindenhurst School District to educate students in the values, critical skills, and essential knowledge necessary to be informed and responsible citizens, prepared to take the next steps in their education, careers and lives in our diverse society. The goal of the District shall be to provide a safe and nurturing environment in which students will be motivated to achieve academic excellence, positive values, and a strong self-image in preparation for a successful future.

The Lindenhurst High School Guidance Department has a goal of increasing the percent of 12th grade students who plan to attend college, specifically four-year colleges, during the 2008–2009 school year.

STEP TWO: ELEMENT

ELEMENT
What critical data element are you trying to impact? (Examples include grades; test scores; attendance; promotion rates; graduation rates; post-secondary-going rate; enrollment into honors or AP courses, special education; discipline referral data; etc.)
What is the baseline for the data element? Where do you hope to move it (goal)?

Element: Percentage of students who plan to continue on to four-year colleges after graduation.
Baseline: 47% of students who applied to continue on in four-year colleges (2006–2007 school year).
50.7% of students who applied to continue on in four-year colleges (2007–2008 school year).
Goal: 53% of students who will apply to continue on in four-year colleges (2008–2009 school year).

STEP THREE: ANALYZE

ANALYZE THE DATA ELEMENT
You can use percentages, averages, raw scores, quartiles, or stanines. You can aggregate or disaggregate the data to better understand which students are meeting success. You can disaggregate by gender, race, ethnicity, socio-economic status, or in a multitude of ways to look at student groupings.

The Baseline Data revealed:
The percentage of 12th grade students who applied to four-year colleges in 2006–2007 and 2008–2009 has been increasing.

Percentage of 12th Grade Students Who Applied to Four-Year College

Post-secondary Options	2006–2007	2007–2008
4-year college	47%	50.7%

STEP FOUR: STAKEHOLDERS-UNITE

STAKEHOLDERS-UNITE TO DEVELOP STRATEGIES TO IMPACT THE DATA ELEMENT

Beginning Date: 9/1/08
Ending Date: 6/26/09

Stakeholders	Strategies
School Counselor(s)	• Gave students the tools they needed to succeed, including help with study skills, counseling services, referrals, and teacher meetings. • Consulted with other stakeholders often to ensure student success. • Encouraged students to enroll in challenging courses. • Utilized data-driven guidance plans to ensure the academic, personal, and social development of all students. • Encouraged participation in after school and volunteer activities. • Participated in college planning meetings, junior conferences, and financial aid workshops. • Guided students through the college application and decision-making process. • Organized college mini-fairs and visitations. • Organized on-site admissions days. • Presented at parent meetings at all levels.
Administrator(s)	• Supported a highly qualified staff to work directly with students. • Ensured a safe learning environment. • Developed new ways of reaching out to parents and students. • Made creative budgeting funds. • Encouraged and evaluated staff to promote high student achievement.
Teachers	• Looked for alternative ways to teach students that supported the many different types of learning styles. • Offered extra help. • Promoted student achievement at all times. • Consulted with other stakeholders.
Students	• Made use of the available resources. • Gifted students offered peer-tutoring programs. • Consulted with school counselors and college admissions counselors to find the college that best fit them.

Stakeholders	Strategies
Parents	• Attended school meetings. • Helped children with their homework. • Helped children study for tests. • Supported the teachers and administrative staff. • Consulted often with teachers and school counselors. • Encouraged children to seek the positive results of a college education. • Participated in junior conferences and after-school college-planning meetings.
Parent Teacher Associations	• Supported the staff and gave ideas on how students could better succeed in an educational setting. • Assisted with parent information sharing. • Supported parent information nights.
School Psychologists	• Ensured the mental and personal/social development of the students. • Ensured that students had outside referral sources if needed. • Evaluated students for special education when needed.
Social Workers	• Ensured the mental and personal/social development of the students. • Ran groups for students in the college application process.
Colleges and Universities	• Offered Regents Review classes, especially in math. • Sent admissions representatives to help students see the varieties of post-secondary options that are available. • Offered college level courses at local high schools.
Resources (grants, technology, etc.)	• Helped facilitate the educational growth of all students.

STEP FIVE: RESULTS

RESULTS

Restate your baseline data.
State where your data is now. Did you meet your goal?

Restate baseline data: Results (data now):   Met Goal: Yes X No ____

Percentage of 12th Grade Students Who Plan to Attend Four-year College

Post-secondary Options	2006–2007	2007–2008	2008–2009
Four-year college	47%	50.7%	55%

Questions to consider as you examine results and revise your MEASURE:

Which strategies had a positive impact on the data?
All of the strategies implemented led to an increase in students who applied to four-year colleges upon graduation to the current rate of 55%.

Which strategies should be replaced, changed, added?
At this time, the only strategy that must be reviewed is the assignment of two counselors to work with all special education students. The district cut one counselor position from the budget for 2009–2010, and it might not be possible to continue this program beyond next year.

Based on what you have learned, how will you revise STEP FOUR, STAKEHOLDERS UNITE?
We will work to keep all counselors informed about a broader range of four-year colleges where our students can be admitted and can qualify for financial aid and merit scholarships. We will examine retraining all counselors to be expert in advising special education students to attend college in the event we must abandon our "special education counselors" approach.

How did your MEASURE contribute to systemic change(s) in your school and/or in your community?
Central office administrators are more aware of the impact of counselors have on the achievement of the district goal of higher number of four-college, post-graduate plans. High school students have a higher awareness of the value of a college education and talk to one another about it more often and more knowledgeably. Parents are better informed about the college admissions and selections process and the importance of financial aid, and parents can support their children as they formulate their post graduate plans. Faculty participate in our college fairs and encourage students to attend college far more than in the past, leading to a school wide initiative emphasizing academic achievement to promote college admissions.

STEP SIX: EDUCATE

Educate others as to your efforts to move data. Show how the work of the school counselor(s) is connected to the mission of the schools and to school achievement.

Additionally, the results of this high school wide initiative have been disseminated through:

- Guidance Advisory Board presentation
- Building Principal information sessions
- Department meeting discussions
- PTA meeting presentation
- Annual Report of Department Coordinator to the Superintendent and Deputy Superintendent
- Board of Education report and presentation
- Inclusion of this data element in our grade-level and college-preparation parent presentations

Lindenhurst High School MEASURE of Success

Principal: Mr. Daniel E. Giordano
School Counselor(s): Ms. Jaime Carey
Enrollment: 2,395

Principal's Comment

I am pleased to see that more of our students are planning to attend a four-year college. Our students work hard and deserve to enjoy the rich college experience found in these schools.

School Counselor(s)'s Comment

Students who attend four-year colleges are more likely to graduate on time and enjoy a more comprehensive college experience. It is a more desirable post-graduate plan for our students.

Critical Data Element(s)

Percent of students who apply to four-year colleges after graduation.

Systemic Changes

All high school counselors encourage junior conferences with parents present.

All parent evening meetings emphasize college admissions and selections information.

All classroom guidance presentations include information about applying to college.

All counselors attend information sessions and/or college tours to improve their knowledge base about four-year colleges.

The department offers three separate parent information meetings about financial aid and applying for scholarships.

Faculty members are involved in our college fairs and classroom guidance presentations on post-secondary planning.

Stakeholders Involved

Counselor(s): Gave students the tools they needed to succeed, including help with study skills, counseling services, referrals, and teacher meetings.
Administrator: Supported a highly qualified staff to work directly with students.

Teachers: Promoted student achievement at all times.
Parents: Consulted often with teachers and school counselors.
Students: Made use of the available resources.

Results

Fifty-five percent of the graduates of 2009 applied to four-year colleges after graduation. Our goal was 53% in 2009.

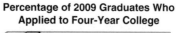

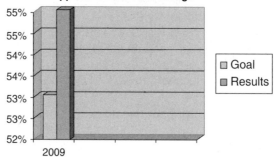

Faces Behind the Data

Geraldo failed to follow up on his application to City University of NY and as a result was denied admission. His counselor contacted an administrator and colleague at a private four-year institution to inquire if they would consider this student's application. As a result of a close cooperative relationship between the admissions office and the counselor, the college agreed to admit the student and additionally awarded a scholarship, which reduced the tuition enough make it comparable to the CUNY tuition. The student will attend this four-year college through the very personalized intervention of his counselor, the coordinator of guidance, and a college partner. Without the advocacy and leadership of this particular intervention, the student would most likely have changed his plans to attend a four-year college.

MEASURE

Mission, Element, Analyze, Stakeholders-Unite, Results, Educate
A Six-step Accountability Process for School Counselors

Name and Address of School:
John Overton Comprehensive High School,
4820 Franklin Road
Nashville, TN 37220

Principal:
Dr. Shuler Pelham

Name of Counselor(s) Leading the Initiative:
Joy Guss, Senior Counselor

Enrollment:
1658

School Demographics:
African American: 35%
Asian/Pacific Islander: 6%
Hispanic/Latina: 18%
Caucasian/Non-Hispanic: 41%
English as Second Language: 17%
Free-Reduced Lunches: 63%
Special Education: 10%

STEP ONE: MISSION

MISSION
Connect your work to your school's mission in keeping with the ASCA or your state's comprehensive school counseling model.

Your school or department's mission statement is:
John Overton High School will provide a rigorous, diverse, and relevant curriculum while maintaining a safe learning environment. Students will gain the knowledge necessary to pass required courses and assessments for graduation and become responsible citizens in our global society.

STEP TWO: ELEMENT

ELEMENT
What critical data element *are you trying to impact? (Examples include grades; test scores; attendance; promotion rates; graduation rates; post-secondary-going rate; enrollment into honors or AP courses, special education; discipline referral data; etc.)*
    What is the baseline *for the data element? Where do you hope to move it* (goal)?

Element: Pass rate for standard Algebra I classes.
Baseline: 2006–2007/2007–2008 standard Algebra I classes—64%/65% pass rates.
Goal: Increase pass rate by 10% to 75% pass rate.

STEP THREE: ANALYZE

ANALYZE THE DATA ELEMENT

You can use percentages, averages, raw scores, quartiles, or stanines. You can aggregate or disaggregate the data to better understand which students are meeting success. You can disaggregate by gender, race, ethnicity, socio-economic status, or in a multitude of ways to look at student groupings.

The Baseline Data revealed:
An unacceptable number of students taking standard Algebra I failed in the fall semester. The 2006–2007 and 2007–2008 pass rates for standard Algebra I were 64% and 65% respectively, while the pass rates for the Honors Algebra I students was 78% in 2006–2007 and 80% in 2007–2008. The discrepancy in pass rates between standard and honors level Algebra I courses showed a critical need for additional interventions in the standard Algebra I courses. Our goal was to expand the opportunity for success to all learners, not just the advanced.

STEP FOUR: STAKEHOLDERS-UNITE

STAKEHOLDERS-UNITE TO DEVELOP STRATEGIES TO IMPACT THE DATA ELEMENT

Beginning Date: School Year 2007–2008 to develop plan/School Year 2008–2009 to actually place tutors in classes.

Ending Date: School Year 2008–2009—program is ongoing.

Stakeholders	Strategies
School Counselor(s)	• Proposed implementation of selective in-school, peer-tutoring program in 2008–2009 school year to address standard Algebra I pass rate. • Planned faculty meeting discussion/planning of program. • Implemented a selective in-school, peer tutoring program for 2008–2009 school year by expanding the Service Learning course to include tutors (in the past Service Learning had been students assigned as office workers only). • Targeted tutors for Algebra I classes. • Recruited rising seniors from high-end Honors and AP math classes during 2007–2008 spring course registration for the 2008–2009 school year. • Required and reviewed applications for potential tutors (applications had to have a teacher recommendation and parent signature) and made final selections. • Placed tutors in standard Algebra I classes for 2008–2009 school year. • Provided training session for tutors. • Solicited feedback/grades for the tutors from the Algebra I teachers. • Monitored the peer-tutoring program. • Collected data to analyze impact.
Administrator(s)	• Analyzed longitudinal data and determined an improvement plan was needed for pass rate in standard Algebra I classes—shared information in faculty/steering committee/school improvement plan meetings. • Approved senior counselor request to expand the Service Learning Program to include peer tutors in standard Algebra I classes to address pass rate. • Service Learning Peer-Tutoring program included in formal school improvement plan.
Teachers	• Provided input during faculty meetings. • Wrote Service Learning Peer Tutors into the School Improvement Plan. • Wrote recommendations for tutors. • Completed grading rubrics for the tutors each nine weeks. • Completed surveys to assess program.

Stakeholders	Strategies
Students	• Applied, obtained letters of recommendation and parent permission, and were interviewed for assignment as tutors. • Completed fall training session with senior counselor. • Completed at least two service projects outside school hours in addition to their tutoring services. • Developed responsibility and service ethic. • Modified honors course electives to have room in schedule for tutoring.
Student Organizations (clubs, teams, etc.)	• Service Learning clubs, such as Interact, helped recruit by spreading the message of service through the role of tutoring.
Parents	• Gave signed permission for students to participate in Service Learning Peer Tutoring program. • Provided supportive role at home.
Colleges and Universities	• Recognized the leadership and service demonstrated by students who are peer tutors at John Overton.
School Improvement Team	• Utilized data on 2006–2007 and 2007–2008 failure rates in standard Algebra I classes to determine a need for more interventions and new approaches to improve pass rates. • Used data on effectiveness of peer tutors to approve an in-school, peer-tutoring program for 2008–2009 school year. • Included an in-school Service Learning Peer-Tutoring program as part of formal School Improvement Plan.

STEP FIVE: RESULTS

RESULTS

Restate your baseline data.
State where your data is now. Did you meet your goal?

Restate baseline data: Results (data now):   Met goal: Yes X No _____

School Year	Standard Algebra I pass rate
2006–2007	64%
2007–2008	65%
2008–2009 (with peer tutors)	78%
2008–2009 (without peer tutors)	67%

*Two 2008–2009 standard Algebra I classes did not have tutors in order to serve as control groups to account for any impact staffing changes may have created to the pass rates.

Questions to Consider as you examine results and revise your MEASURE:

Which strategies had a positive impact on the data?
• Faculty input. Teacher buy-in was critical to the success of the program.
• Recruiting tutors from high-end math courses to tutor students in lower-level math courses. In anecdotal notes, some teachers have written that the tutors are an essential component in the success of the students—and an essential part of their classrooms, comparable to student teachers.
• Making students apply and get teacher recommendations and parent permission to participate in the program. This helped ensure tutors were both highly qualified and highly motivated to be peer tutors.
• Including Service Learning Peer Tutoring in the formal School Improvement Plan. This provided an added layer of accountability.
• Keeping control groups in the current year helped neutralize the difference staffing changes may have made to the rates, and show the true impact the tutors are making in classrooms.

Which strategies should be replaced, changed, added?
- More regular, periodic training of the tutors could enhance their skills.
- Regular sessions for the tutors to meet as a group and provide feedback and tips to each other. Some tutors were frustrated when students they were helping did not understand or did not seem motivated to improve. Periodic "venting" sessions could give them strategies to deal with frustrations.
- Expanding the tutoring program to include other required courses, especially Gateway tested courses, would be of benefit to our school.

Based on what you have learned, how will you revise Step Four "Stakeholders-Unite?"
- Including additional staff at school in the recruitment and management of the tutors will be essential to expand the program beyond its current level. The other counselors are excited about recruiting juniors they work with, and our Leadership Teacher is interested in merging her class with Service Learning.

How did your MEASURE contribute to systemic change(s) in your school and/or in your community?
- More students are passing Algebra I, a required math course for every student in high school.
- There has been a paradigm shift from Service Learning being an "easy" elective (office workers only) to Service Learning being an essential part of our school. Teachers are actively asking how the program can be expanded to include tutors for more subjects, translators for ELL courses, and suggesting students to recruit as tutors.
- Our steering committee, comprised of the administrative team and all the department heads, is discussing assigning Service Learning to a full-time teacher, and including a Service Learning/Leadership SLC Path for the new state graduation requirements. We currently have a Leadership teacher who is interested in becoming more involved with the Service Learning program. A full-time teacher would be able to provide more regular training and support sessions to the tutors, thereby enhancing the effectiveness of the program. Counselors could continue to be involved in recruitment, data collection, consultative services, and training sessions.
- More Scholars Path students are showing an interest in Service Learning. In the past, Scholars Path students typically filled their course schedules with all AP and Honors academic courses. Seeing high achieving students replace an Honors/AP credit with Service Learning to provide a needed service to their school has been truly inspiring. Our school's mission statement includes helping students become more responsible citizens. This helps meet that goal.
- More diverse students interact and are exposed to each other in positive ways. Often, the Honors/AP students have little to no interaction with the students in standard courses, and vice-versa. By interacting and helping one another, bridges have been built to increase understanding and tolerance among the diverse groups represented in our school population.

STEP SIX: EDUCATE

Educate others concerning efforts to move data. Develop a report card that shows how the work of the school counselor(s) is connected to the mission of the schools and to student success. Below is an example of a report card.

John Overton Comprehensive High School MEASURE of Success

Principal: Dr. Shuler Pelham
School Counselor(s): Joy Guss, Senior Counselor
Enrollment: 1658

Principal's Comment

The idea of expanding the role of Service Learning to incorporate student peer tutors in high-needs courses and classes such as Algebra I has been tremendous. I attribute one of the most important reasons for the success to the dedication of our counseling staff and administration to preserving the integrity of the idea. Counselors were very selective about which students were recruited and allowed to participate, and this ensured teacher buy-in and a positive formation of the initial vision. Incorporating this into our development of an SLC pathway in leadership will provide a great opportunity to expand this culture of community service that is already very strong in our school.

School Counselor(s)'s Comment

Implementing a peer tutoring program has been one of the most exciting things I have done as a high school counselor. It has been successful beyond my wildest dreams, taking on a life of its own. It has been well worth the time and effort involved to get it implemented.

Critical Data Element(s)

Improve the pass rate for standard Algebra I classes.

Systemic Changes

Collaboration efforts with administrators, teachers, counselors, steering committee and school improvement plan committee members resulted in a school wide, in-school Service Learning Peer-Tutoring program. The target for 2008–2009 was standard Algebra I classes. Beginning with the 2009–2010 school year, an entire Service Learning/Leadership SLC pathway with a focus on in-school tutoring, translating and assisting in classes will be implemented.

Stakeholders Involved

Counselor(s): Implemented in-school service learning peer tutoring program in standard Algebra I classes.
Administrator: Gave the green-light for the program and valuable input as to where the tutors should initially be placed.

Teachers: Completed pre-program surveys, allowed tutors to be placed in their classrooms, graded tutors, and provided valuable feedback on the success/progress of the program.
Parents: Gave permission for students to participate and supported the efforts of the school to help students pass Algebra I.
Students: Were willing to apply, get recommendations, attend trainings, and work as tutors for one period each day.

Results

School Year	Standard Algebra I pass rate	Honors Algebra I pass rate
2006–2007	64%	78%
2007–2008	65%	80%
2008–2009 (classes with peer tutors)	78%	NA
2008–2009 (classes without peer tutors)	67%	74%

Peer tutoring was implemented during the 2008–2009 school year.

Pass rate for Standard Algebra I classes with tutors (78%) actually exceeds the pass rate for Honors Algebra I classes (74%) for 2008–2009 school year.

Faces Behind the Data

Anthony, a struggling freshman, said of the student tutor in his Algebra I class, "Raymond would explain some things better than the teacher did to me. He used good examples, and helped out when I needed it. I liked having him in there." Anthony passed Algebra I at the end of the semester. When asked if having a student tutor helped him pass, Anthony responded, "Most definitely!"

Chaney, who is a National Merit Scholar, had a gap in his senior schedule, and followed my suggestion that he become a tutor in an Algebra I class. In the spring, when asked about his experience tutoring, he said at first it was a little strange walking into a room full of freshman. But he soon began to connect, adding that he's glad to have "become a part of what they need."

MEASURE

Mission, Element, Analyze, Stakeholders-Unite, Results, Educate
A Six-step Accountability Process for School Counselors

Name and Address of School:
Sheffield Elementary School
4290 Chuck Avenue
Memphis, TN 38118

Principal:
Vanessa Wesley

Name of Counselor(s) Leading the Initiative:
Annie Grays

Enrollment:
446

School Demographics:
Caucasian/Non-Hispanic: .4%
Hispanic: 13.1%
African American: 85.8%
Asian/Pacific Islander: .2%
Other: .4%
Free-Reduced Lunch: 96.3%

STEP ONE: MISSION

MISSION
Connect your work to your school's mission in keeping with the ASCA or your state's comprehensive school counseling model.

Your school or department's mission statement is:
Our mission is to educate all students to their highest potential by preparing minds early.

STEP TWO: ELEMENT

ELEMENT
What critical data element are you trying to impact? (Examples include grades; test scores; attendance; promotion rates; graduation rates; post-secondary-going rate; enrollment into honors or AP courses, special education; discipline referral data; etc.)
*   What is the baseline for the data element? Where do you hope to move it (goal)?*

Element 1: Attendance Rate.
Baseline 1: Attendance Rate 92.6% (2006).
Goal 1: Increase attendance rate from 92.6% (2006) to 93.0% (2008).

Element 2: Promotion Rate.
Baseline 2: Promotion Rate 85.2% (2006).
Goal 2: Increase promotion rate from 85.2% (2006) to 86.0% (2008).

STEP THREE: ANALYZE

ANALYZE THE DATA ELEMENT

You can use percentages, averages, raw scores, quartiles, or stanines. You can aggregate or disaggregate the data to better understand which students are meeting success. You can disaggregate by gender, race, ethnicity, socio-economic status, or in a multitude of ways to look at student groupings.

The Baseline Data revealed:

	2006
Attendance Rate	92.6%
Promotion Rate	85.2%

STEP FOUR: STAKEHOLDERS-UNITE

STAKEHOLDERS-UNITE TO DEVELOP STRATEGIES TO IMPACT THE DATA ELEMENT

Beginning Date: 9/6/09
Ending Date: 06/20/09

Stakeholders	Strategies
School Counselor(s)	• Analyzed data from 2006 from the Tennessee School Report Card & Critical Data Elements (Attendance and Promotion Rates). • Organized and planned a Guidance Advisory Team that assisted in the planning and implementation. • Planned and conducted parent sessions to enhance support for student achievement and improve attendance. • Monitored social progress of selected students and reassessed cases as needed. • Assisted staff in identifying and implementing appropriate interventions through the S-Team Process. • Organized and implemented specific interventions for those students who were referred during Support Team meetings. • Provided classroom guidance on the importance of attendance and promotion. • Kept staff updated on school-wide attendance efforts and progress. • Identified and provided group counseling for those requiring extra academic support or motivation to perform. • Identified those retained last year and met with them periodically to assess current academic status. • Assisted and supported the SART (Student Attendance Review Team) meetings for improved attendance. • Supported monitoring of the 20-day attendance.
Administrator(s)	• Encouraged staff adherence to the attendance policy and Quality First Teaching to increase promotion and attendance rates. • Requested that staff make appropriate attendance and achievement referrals. • Communicated with staff concerning the importance of attendance. • Provided school-wide incentives for attendance. • Identified SART for school. • Supported and monitored implementation of interventions to improve targets.
Teachers	• Adhered to the District's policy for reporting absenteeism. • Referred child to SART if child had too many absences (excused or unexcused). • Turned in all excuses. • Motivated children concerning attendance by providing incentives for the class or individual. • Notified counselor after the first six weeks if student(s) were not performing on or near grade level. • Referred all concerns suspected to contribute to absenteeism. • Participated in all Student Support Team meetings on referred students.

Stakeholders	Strategies
School Psychologists	• Supported the Student Support Team process. • Administered evaluations. • Assisted in academic, behavioral, and social development planning and interventions.
School Social Worker	• Conducted small group sessions with children experiencing similar concerns that could contribute to poor performance. • Supported the Student Support Team process (i.e., Behavioral Planning, ADHD Evaluations). • Assisted in academic, behavioral, and social development planning and interventions.
Clerical Staff	• Supported the distribution of correspondence to parents per attendance policy. • Managed daily attendance database.
Colleges and Universities	• Read to selected groups during library time.
School Clubs	• Organized committee of volunteers to head school clubs and organizations. • Encouraged participation in the Jr. Beta Club, Peer Mediation, Book Club, Student Leadership, and Black History poetry contests.
Parents	• Supported the school's efforts. • Participated in parent meetings concerning attendance and promotion. • Contacted Parent Advocate for needs that could be a contributing factor for poor attendance and promotional efforts. • Attended school-wide activities and visited their child's classroom. • Monitored attendance and grades.
Volunteers	• Obtained necessary screening documents. • Met with principal or designee concerning placement. • *Our Children—Our Future* volunteers worked with two students, twice per week.
Business Partners	• Helped provide incentives for attendance and promotion. • Spoke at selected parent meetings. • Spoke at selected student gatherings.
Community Agencies	• Provided appropriate services for specific cases outside of the school (i.e., Southeast Mental Health Center).
Instructional Facilitator	• Provided testing data to analyze strengths and weaknesses. • Participated in Student Support Team meetings to help brainstorm interventions. • Helped provide attendance and promotional encouragement. • Trained teachers on classroom strategies and findings that promote learning.
Literacy Leader	• Provided DIBELS evaluation data for intervention planning. • Participated in some Student Support Team meetings, and assisted in planning interventions.
Parent Advocate	• Communicated with parents of students who were continuously off task and/or hindering learning in the classroom. • Planned and conducted parent meetings, especially Title I.
Students	• Became involved in various clubs and organizations. • Signed Academic and Behavioral COMPACT (pledge). • Made self-referrals.
Technology	• Used technology to disaggregate, access, compile and display data.
Media Specialist	• Assisted in making audio/visual equipment available when needed. • Displayed and/or made books available to coincide with themes of classroom guidance. • Assisted with attendance incentives for classrooms.
Attendance Teacher	• Served as school-home liaison by meeting with the school weekly to address attendance and tardiness issues. • Made home investigations to inform parents of children referred due to poor attendance, tardiness, early and late pick-ups, and explained the attendance policy. • Provided necessary follow-up and made referrals when necessary to Juvenile Court.

STEP FIVE: RESULTS

RESULTS

Restate your baseline data.
State where your data is now. Did you meet your goal?

Restate baseline data: Results (data now):   Met Goal: Yes X No _____

	2006	2007	2008	2009	TN DOE Goal
Attendance Rate	92.6%	93.5%	93.6%	91.5%	93.0%
Promotion Rate	85.2%	88.3%	88.8%	96%	97%

Questions to Consider as you examine results and revise your MEASURE:

Which strategies had a positive impact on the data?
Support from administration made a tremendous impact on the results.

Which strategies should be replaced, changed, added?
None. Everything seemed to work. We will continue to monitor.

Based on what you have learned, how will you revise Step Four "Stakeholders-Unite?"
We will increase the number of agencies we connect with.

How did your MEASURE contribute to systemic change(s) in your school and/or in your community?
Strategies seemed to have worked to improve the target areas.

STEP SIX: EDUCATE

Educate others as to your efforts to move data. Develop a report card that shows how the work of the school counselor(s) is connected to the mission of the schools and to student success. Below is an example of a report card.

Sheffield Elementary School MEASURE of Success

Principal: Mrs. Vanessa Wesley
School Counselor(s): Annie Greys
Enrollment: 455

Principal's Comment

The SART team made a tremendous, positive impact on our attendance last year with the school counselor (Annie Grays) and ISS (Rev. Gillespie).
I hope the impact continues in the future.

School Improvement Issues

Poor attendance can impact performance, and ultimately the promotion rate.
School-wide activities, clubs, involvement, and academic success can help increase attendance.

Critical Data Element(s)

Attendance and promotion rate

Systemic Changes

Attendance
As a result of the collaboration among stakeholders, the entire staff seems motivated to boost attendance.

Promotion Rate
The teachers are consulting with the principal and counselor as soon as they realize that a child needs more help to succeed academically.

Stakeholders Involved

Counselor: Planned efforts to improve attendance and promote academic success.
Teachers: Supported the counselor's efforts in improving the attendance and promotion rate.
Parents: Worked with the school in the planning and implementation.
Students: Encouraged parents to get them to school on time and worked hard in their classes and on their tests.
Administrator: Provided support, leadership, Incentives, etc. for the implementation of the program.

Office and School Support Staff: Provided proper documents and letters to parents.
Community Stakeholders: Worked extensively with the school by providing incentives and support.

Results

	2006	2007	2008	2009	TN DOE Goal
Attendance Rate	92.6%	93.5%	93.6%	91.5%	93.0%
Promotion Rate	85.2%	88.3%	88.8%	96%	97.0%

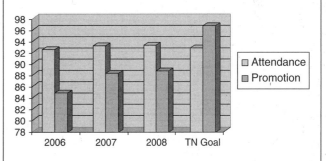

Faces Behind the Data

"T", a 3rd grader, who was chronically late to school, never seemed to mind that she missed the first hour of the Reading Block every day. We finally were able to get her parents and the little girl to meet with us one morning, later than the start time (of course). "T" said she didn't like coming late every day and missing reading time. Her mother said, "We're going to turn things around". She told us she wasn't at home when T left for school. Mom was able to change her hours within a short period of time and "T" was not late once the rest of the school year."

MEASURE

**Mission, Element, Analyze, Stakeholders-Unite, Results, Educate
A Six-step Accountability Process for School Counselors**

Name and Address of School:
Sweet Apple Elementary School
12025 Etris Road
Roswell, GA 30075

Principal:
Lenny Forti

Name of Counselor(s) Leading the Initiative:
Lynn Haldaman and Tom Perrine

Enrollment:
899

School Demographics:
Asian/Pacific Islander: 6.8%
African American: 6.9%
Hispanic/Latino: 2%
Caucasian/Non-Hispanic: 80%
Multiracial: 4.3%
LEP: 0.6%
Economically Disadvantaged: 4.7%
Special Education: 15.6%

STEP ONE: MISSION

MISSION
Connect your work to your school's mission in keeping with the ASCA or your state's comprehensive school counseling model.

Your school or department's mission statement is:
The Sweet Apple community will collaborate to prepare all students for the future. It is our mission to provide a strong foundation in academics, high expectations for citizenship, cultural arts experiences, and a safe, nurturing environment.

STEP TWO: ELEMENT

ELEMENT
What critical data element are you trying to impact? (Examples include grades test scores; attendance; promotion rates; graduation rates; post-secondary-going rate; enrollment into honors or AP courses, special education; discipline referral data, and so on.)
    What is the baseline for the data element? Where do you hope to move it (goal)?

Elements: Criterion-Reference Competency Test (CRCT) Scores.
Baseline: On the basis of performance on the Spring 2008 CRCT, 37 students in grades 2 through 5 are deemed to be at-risk not to meet expectations on the Reading and/or Math portions of the Spring 2009 CRCT.
Goal: 50% of students in grades 2 through 5 who did not meet expectations (Level 1) on the 2008 CRCT will at least increase to Level 2 on the 2009 CRCT.

STEP THREE: ANALYZE

ANALYZE THE DATA ELEMENT

You can use percentages, averages, raw scores, quartiles, or stanines. You can aggregate or disaggregate the data to better understand which students are meeting success. You can disaggregate by gender, race, ethnicity, socio-economic status, or in a multitude of ways to look at student groupings.

Baseline Data Revealed:
CRCT performance indicates that 37 students in grades 2 through 5 scored at Level 1 on the 2008 CRCT in reading or math or both.

STEP FOUR: STAKEHOLDERS-UNITE

STAKEHOLDERS-UNITE TO DEVELOP STRATEGIES TO IMPACT THE DATA ELEMENT

Beginning Date: October 2008
Ending Date: April 2009

Stakeholders	Strategies
School Counselor(s)	• Conducted pre and post needs assessments for all CRCT Level 1 students. • Worked with Level 1 students, individually and in small groups, to develop academic skills, self-advocacy skills, self-concept, and goal setting; tracked academic progress of group members throughout the year. • Provided regular feedback to parents of group members.
EIP and IRR Teachers	• Provided ratings of group members and provided feedback on academic and social progress of group members. • Supported the ideas of the plan.
Classroom Teachers	• Provided ratings of group members and provided feedback on academic progress of group members. • Provided opportunities for counselors to meet with students. • Supported the ideas of the plan.
Administrators	• Supported and encouraged staff in this program, particularly since it was closely tied to the school's strategic plan. • Worked with Level 1 students, individually and in small groups, to develop academic skills, self-advocacy skills, self-concept, and goal setting; tracked academic progress of group members throughout the year.
Parents	• Provided encouragement and support to students. • Monitored student grades. • Implemented strategies suggested by counselors.
Students	• Participated in small groups, as well as individual conferencing, with counselors and administrators. • Used strategies they were taught to enhance academic performance. • Talked with administrative mentor regarding ideas that might increase scores and set goals.

STEP FIVE: RESULTS

RESULTS

Restate your baseline data.
State where your data are now. Did you meet your goal?

Restate baseline data: Results (data now):   Met Goal: Yes X No ____

	Grade 2		Grade 3		Grade 4		Grade 5	
Year	**Reading**	**Math**	**Reading**	**Math**	**Reading**	**Math**	**Reading**	**Math**
2008	2	2	2	5	3	16	2	12
2009	0	2	2	3	1	6	1	4

Table heading: Level 1 Students

Questions to consider as you examine results and revise your MEASURE:

Which strategies had a positive impact on the data?
Six members of the administrative team each worked with 6–8 of these students, checking on their progress throughout the school year, meeting with students individually and in small groups, and also contacting parents and teachers periodically.

Which strategies should be replaced, changed, added?
We probably will not give our principal a group of students next year, due to all his other responsibilities. We may consider a checklist of activities for the administrators to use to be sure they are checking on our level-one students regularly so that all students receive approximately the same interventions.

STEP SIX: EDUCATE

Educate others as to your efforts to move data. Develop a report card that shows how the work of the school counselor(s) is connected to the mission of the schools and to student success. Below is an example of a report card.

Sweet Apple Elementary School MEASURE of Success

Principal: Lenny Forti
School Counselor(s): Lynn Haldaman and Tom Perrine
Enrollment: 899

Principal's Comment

One of the major goals of our school's 2008–2009 Strategic Plan was to target low-performing students in the areas of language arts and mathematics. There were 37 students, returning to our school this year, who fell below state minimum CRCT standards in these two academic areas. Our school plan, which included the guidance plan, addressed specific strategies to raise student performance either to meet or exceed state standards. Strategies included using the administrative team to mentor and monitor this group throughout the school year, providing testing feedback and planning time for classroom teachers, counselors working with students in small groups, and increased parent communication. Results from spring CRCT administration showed a significant improvement in the scores of these identified students. The collaborative efforts of parents, teachers and administrators have positively contributed to the success of our students. Strategies from this year's plan will be evaluated over the summer months, and modifications will be made to address the continued improvement of low-performing students at our school.

School Counseling's Comment

We were particularly challenged this past year to assist our students to improve their confidence and skills in math. The state's math curriculum was completely changed beginning with the 2007–2008 school year. Employing the "MEASURE" approach has helped us enlarge our team so that students might receive the support they need to be successful.

Critical Data Element(s)

Criterion-Reference Competency Test (CRCT) Scores.

Systemic Changes

All level 1 students worked in small groups where they were challenged to develop their academic and self-advocacy skills, self concept, and goal setting. There was an increase in teacher, administrator, and parent collaboration.

Stakeholders Involved

Counselor(s): Worked with Level 1 students individually and in small groups to develop academic skills, self-advocacy skills, self-concept, and goal setting; tracked academic progress of group members throughout the year.
Administrator: Supported and encouraged staff in this program, particularly since it was closely tied to the school's strategic plan.
Teachers: Supported the ideas of the plan.
Parents: Implemented strategies suggested by counselors.
Students: Used strategies they were taught to enhance academic performance.

Results

Thirty-seven students in grades 2–5 scored Level 1 in reading/math or both on the 2008 CRCT. 9 students scored Level 1 in reading and 35 students scored Level 1 in math. On the 2009 CRCT, 4 students scored Level 1 in reading, (a reduction of 56%) and 15 students scored Level 1 in math (a reduction of 57%) grades 2–5.

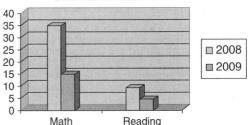

Level 1 Score on CRCT Students Grades 2–5

Faces Behind the Data

One of the many strategies we used was small group work involving the students and the two school counselors. One administrator decided to take on a small group herself. She met with a group of seven 5th-grade, special education boys for lunch once a week from January through March and called it the "Math Club." She gave them challenging math problems to complete and bring back to her before the next club meeting. The boys felt very special, and all but one met the state-level expectations on the math section of the CRCT. Our administrator really enjoyed getting to know these boys better and really looked forward to the special time for "Math Club." They all were proud of their accomplishments.

MEASURE

Mission, Element, Analyze, Stakeholders-Unite, Results, Educate
A Six-step Accountability Process for School Counselors

Name and Address of School:
West Haven High School
1 McDonough Plaza
West Haven, CT 06516

Principal:
Mr. Ronald Stancil

Name of Counselor(s) Leading the Initiative:
Rose A. Paolino, Ed.D., Department Chair; Cathy Bednarz; Holly Benedetti; Heather Doraz; Robert Jeffords; Norma Merced; Heather Patch; Intern: Stephanie Seligmann

Enrollment:
1,588

School Demographics:
Caucasian/Non-Hispanic: 50%
African American: 26%
Hispanic: 20%
Asian/Pacific Islander: 3.5%
Native American: 0.5%
Free-Reduced Lunch: 45%
English as Second Language: 3%
Exceptional Student Education/Special Education: 8%

STEP ONE: MISSION

MISSION
Connect your work to your school's mission in keeping with the ASCA or your state's comprehensive school counseling model.

Your school or department's mission statement is:
Commit to an education that promotes critical thinking, communication, and problem solving. *Advocate* the development of student talent, as well as collaboration with parents and the local community. *Reinforce* the values of mutual respect, courtesy, and diversity. *Encourage* students to develop responsibility, accountability and self-discipline.

West Haven High School Counseling Department's Mission Statement is aligned with the school's mission statement. School Counselors provide all students with a comprehensive school counseling program that facilitates student growth and development in academic, career, and personal/social domains. We are committed to students as well as working in collaboration with parents, businesses, and community resources to foster optimal student growth.

STEP TWO: ELEMENT

ELEMENT
What critical data element are you trying to impact? (Examples include grades; test scores; attendance; promotion rates; graduation rates; post-secondary-going rate; enrollment into honors or AP courses, special education; discipline referral data; and so on.)
What is the baseline for the data element? Where do you hope to move it (goal)?

Elements: Grades and the number of in-school suspensions.
Baseline:

	June 2006	June 2007	June 2008
% of Freshman Who Failed One or More Academic Courses	41%	33%	38%
Number of In-School Suspensions	2102	2047	1521

Goal: 1. Increase the number of grade 9 students passing their four major academic subjects by 5%.
2. Decrease the number of in-school suspensions by 8%.

STEP THREE: ANALYZE

ANALYZE THE DATA ELEMENT
You can use percentages, averages, raw scores, quartiles, or stanines. You can aggregate or disaggregate the data to better understand which students are meeting success. You can disaggregate by gender, race, ethnicity, socio-economic status, or in a multitude of ways to look at student groupings.

Baseline Data Revealed:
Freshman failure rate, although decreased for one year, went back up in 2007–2008. Suspensions were improving but remained very high.

STEP FOUR: STAKEHOLDERS-UNITE

STAKEHOLDERS-UNITE TO DEVELOP STRATEGIES TO IMPACT THE DATA ELEMENT

Beginning Date: September 2008
Ending Date: June 2009

Stakeholders	Strategies
School Counselor(s)	• Expanded the Counselor/Student Intervention Program (CSI) to all grades. • Presented program and results at faculty meeting.
Administrator(s)	• Utilized program prior to discipline. • Promoted referrals to CSI. • Supported the expansion of the program to include all grades. • Chaperoned class visitations to outside agencies with students assigned to social skills group. • Gave presentation to the Board of Education with the program's results and its impact on reducing in-school suspension rates.
Teachers	• Utilized program when academic, social/personal concerns with students arose, and provided feedback for evaluation.
Student Organizations (clubs, teams, etc.)	• Peer Advocates served as Peer Mentors and Peer Mediators when conflict arose between students. • Peer-tutoring program was used for academic needs.
Parents	• Referred child for support.
School Psychologists	• Served as support personnel for students when referrals were made.
Social Workers	• Served as support personnel. • Offered small group interventions when many students faced a common issue of concern.
Community Agency Members	• Supported students referred to the program by providing information on the Community Teen Club. • School Youth Officers met individually with students.

Stakeholders	Strategies
School Improvement Team	• Supported counselor/student intervention program aligned with objectives of the School Improvement Plan. • Involved School Counseling Department Chair as a member of the team.
Resources (grants, technology, etc.)	• Used a telephone, computer, and printer for NAVIANCE career exploration program. • Used Excel for data disaggregation.

STEP FIVE: RESULTS

RESULTS

Restate your baseline data.
State where your data are now. Did you meet your goal?

Restate baseline data: Results (data now):   Met Goal 1 (Academic): Yes X No ____
Met Goal 2 (In-School Suspensions): Yes X No ____

	June 2006	June 2007	June 2008	June 2009
% of Freshman Who Failed One or More Academic Courses	41%	33%	38%	32%
Number of In-School Suspensions	2102	2047	1521	1215

STEP SIX: EDUCATE

Educate others as to your efforts to move data. Develop a report card that shows how the work of the school counselor(s) is connected to the mission of the schools and to student success. Below is an example of a report card.

West Haven High School MEASURE of Success

Principal: Ronald Stancil
Provost: Kurt Ogren
School Counselor(s): Dr. Rose Paolino, Department Chair; Cathy Bednarz; Holly Benedetti; Heather Doraz; Robert Jeffords; Norma Merced; Heather Patch; and Stephanie Seligmann, Intern
Enrollment: 1588

Provost's Comment

The data clearly demonstrates the positive impact our CSI Program is having on the climate of WHHS, being a tremendous asset particularly to our students in grade nine. The CSI Program is used as a positive intervention to correct negative behavior. It is not punitive in nature; therefore, the referred students are spending more time in their classes and less time in ISS or serving in OSS. I believe the reduction in the suspension rate has a direct correlation to the increase in promotion rate of freshmen. Our students and teachers have benefited greatly from this initiative instituted by our school counseling department.

School Counseling Department Chair's Comment

This initiative demonstrates the efficacy of the comprehensive school counseling program model and the leadership role that school counselors play in positively affecting the academic, career and personal/social development of students. With the support and collaboration of administrators and faculty, the strategies implemented during the last three years increased the percentage of freshmen passing by 3% and decreased the in-school suspension rate by 13.5%.

Critical Data Element(s)

Decreasing the freshmen failure rate and in-school suspensions.

Systemic Changes

Faculty has a better understanding of the school counseling program and services available to students. Parents and students have a greater understanding of the support services available at West Haven High School. Although the freshmen failure rate has decreased minimally, the collection of data from the school counseling department within the last five years has prompted a strong, systematic approach. During the 2008–2009 school year, all freshmen were placed on teams to individualize and personalize their transition to high school. As predicted, this *team concept* fostered an increase in academic achievement and development of social skills.

Stakeholders Involved

Counselors: Reviewed program components and data from the previous year and developed strategies to simplify the referral process and work systematically with all support staff. A social skills group was initiated in addition to a study skills group.
Administrators: Referred students to the CSI Program as a proactive approach to academic and personal/social growth. The Provost, who oversees discipline of all students, was a significant supporter.
Parents: Communicated regarding attendance and referrals.
Social Workers: Supported student referrals in need of social work intervention.
Students: Although 74% of the referrals were freshmen, upper classman who were referred became engaged in the program's goals. One senior wrote an article for the school newspaper, advertising the program and its benefits to students.
Teachers: Utilized program when academic, social/personal concerns with students arose and provided feedback for evaluation.

Results

Academic:
June 2006 = 41% failed one or more academic classes
June 2007 = 33% failed one or more academic classes
June 2008 = 38% failed one or more academic classes
June 2009 = 32% failed one or more academic classes

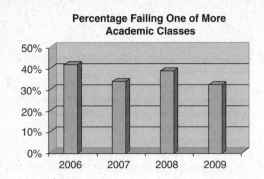

Percentage Failing One of More Academic Classes

In-School Suspensions:

June 2006 = 2047 in-school suspensions (prior to CSI Program implementation)

June 2007 = 1666 in-school suspensions (14% decrease)

June 2008 = 1521 in-school suspensions (9.4% decrease)

June 2009 = 1215 in-school suspensions (13.5% decrease)

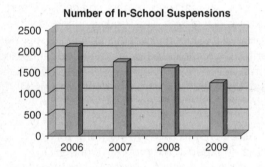

Number of In-School Suspensions

Faces Behind the Data

Student 1: "I was asked to come to the CSI Program by my teacher. I was in an argument and got into in the hallway. My friend and I were having a conversation when I was rudely interrupted. So basically another student tried to get loud with me when he was never in the conversation in the first place. We exchanged some harsh words, and he got sent one way. I know that if I get sent to the Provost one more time I will be suspended and I don't want to be suspended. I wrote my goal after the CSI meeting, which is:

To walk away when someone interrupts me. I want to make honors for at least two marking periods. I will work with my counselor, so I do not get suspended."

"I followed through after my CSI meeting and was not sent to the Provost again. I made honors for one marking period and did not fail any classes for the year." -10th grade student

Student 2: "I was sent down to the CSI counselor by the Provost because me and a friend that has science were about to walk in and the teacher just came out screaming at us saying we're not sitting next to each other. We did not even do anything. We just came in and said what are you talking about and she said you were talking yesterday and we were just like everyone else talking."

"My goal was: to sit where I should sit, not talk, hand my homework in directly to the teacher and meet with my counselor to help me with my grades. I never had to go back to the Provost. I met my goal and passed science for the year." -9th grade student

MEASURE

**Mission, Element, Analyze, Stakeholders-Unite, Results, Educate
A Six-step Accountability Process for School Counselors**

Name and Address of School:
Westmoreland Elementary School
3012 Thompson Lane
Westmoreland, TN 37186

Principal:
Linda Cash

Name of Counselor(s) Leading the Initiative:
Emily Jenkins

Enrollment:
421

School Demographics:
Caucasian/Non-Hispanic: 97.9%
African American: 1.4%
Hispanic: 0.7%
Free-Reduced Lunch: 50.1%

STEP ONE: MISSION

MISSION
Connect your work to your school's mission in keeping with the ASCA or your state's comprehensive school counseling model.

Your school's mission statement is:
Westmoreland Elementary School will educate all children by providing a safe and positive learning environment, while building an educational and technological foundation that will prepare the students for the future. As the family, community and school embrace common goals, student motivation, and success will emerge.

STEP TWO: ELEMENT

ELEMENT
What critical data element are you trying to impact? (Examples include grades; test scores; attendance; promotion rates; graduation rates; post-secondary-going rate; enrollment into honors or AP courses, special education; discipline referral data; etc.)
   What is the baseline *for the data element? Where do you hope to move it* (goal)?

Element: TCAP scores.
Baseline: 94% Proficient in Reading and Language Arts.
Goal 1: Increase the number of students scoring Proficient in Reading/Language Arts.
         TCAP test by increasing "positive" parental/family involvement in school activities.
Goal 2: Continue to improve communication between home and school to promote parental involvement.

STEP THREE: ANALYZE

ANALYZE THE DATA ELEMENT
You can use percentages, averages, raw scores, quartiles, or stanines. You can aggregate or disaggregate the data to better understand which students are meeting success. You can disaggregate by gender, race, ethnicity, socio-economic status, or in a multitude of ways to look at student groupings.

The Baseline Data revealed:
94% student proficiency in Reading and Language Arts.

STEP FOUR: STAKEHOLDERS-UNITE

STAKEHOLDERS-UNITE TO DEVELOP STRATEGIES TO IMPACT THE DATA ELEMENT

Beginning Date: May 2006
Ending Date: May 2008

Stakeholders	Strategies
School Counselor(s)	• Implemented programs such as "Three for Me" Volunteer Program, Boo Hoo Breakfast, Parenting Classes, Career Day, Monthly Character Newsletters, Character Words on School Marquee, and Grandparents Day Family Photos/Lunch. • Served as a parent/staff liaison to ensure that students received a personalized educational experience.
Administrator(s)	• Promoted activities to teachers/staff and parents. Supported and helped fund service project opportunities. • Acted as a liaison between teachers/staff and parents.

Teachers	• Began moving from "normal" parties to educational/informative parties, where students performed and teachers "taught" parents literacy skills.
	  • K-Family Fun Day, Cookout, Bunny Day
	  • Celebrate Reading Picnic
	  • Quantum Learning Challenges, PTO performances
	  • Holiday Plays, PTO performances
	  • K-4 Multicultural Fair, Science Fair, Career Day, Fall Festival
	• Made weekly, positive, parental phone calls.
	• Developed classroom web page.

Students	• Participated in activities that fostered parental involvement and built character. • Actively encouraged families to participate and support school events and activities.
Parents	• Promoted and supported events such as PTO Family Skate Night, field trips, Career Day, Multicultural Fair and the Science Fair. • Helped with Teacher Appreciation volunteers. • Completed climate surveys at the end of the year.
Community Agency Members	• Gallatin Skate Center and Westmoreland Public Library participated in Career Day.
Student Organizations (clubs, teams, etc.)	• FFA and BETA clubs participated in Career Day. • BETA club assisted with Fall Festival.
Other Support Staff (front office, custodial, cafeteria)	• Promoted positive school climate through daily phone and personal interactions with parents and community members. • Provided refreshments and meals to volunteers who participated in W.E.S. events.
Title I Program	• Facilitated parent meetings promoting literacy skills.
Web Resource	• Website which informed parents and community members of upcoming events.

STEP FIVE: RESULTS

RESULTS

Restate your baseline data.
State where your data is now. Did you meet your goal?

Restate baseline data: 94%   Results (data now): 100%   Met Goal: Yes X No _____

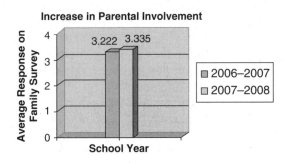

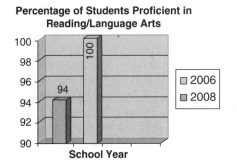

Questions to Consider as you examine results and revise your MEASURE:

Which strategies had a positive impact on the data?
Many of the strategies affected our success within this MEASURE. Educational/informative parties, where students performed and teachers "taught" parents literacy skills was one of the most effective strategies. Also, I believe the Title I promoting literacy skills at parent meetings and the maintenance of a school website informed parents and community members and gave ownership of school events. The implementation of programs such as "Three for Me" Volunteer Program, Boo Hoo Breakfast, Career Day, Monthly Character Newsletters, and Grandparents Day Family Photos/Lunch also positively impacted the data.

Which strategies should be replaced, changed, added?
We would like to add a TCAP informational meeting for parents of 3rd–5th graders. This meeting would outline and review the levels of TCAP proficiency as well as test taking tips.

Based on what you have learned, how will you revise Step Four "Stakeholders-Unite?"
We would begin narrowing the focus to specific, targeted, at-risk groups, refining ways to help parents tutor their children as well as gaining their support for our child-centered environment.

How did your MEASURE contribute to systemic change(s) in your school and/or in your community?
Parents, students, and teachers became part of the intervention and change of the school climate as well as an increase in positive parental involvement. Families also found a medium through which to become active participants in the school and began to feel more comfortable asking questions about student learning and testing.

STEP SIX: EDUCATE

Educate others as to your efforts to move data. Develop a report card that shows how the work of the school counselor(s) is connected to the mission of the schools and to student success. Below is an example of a report card.

Westmoreland Elementary School MEASURE of Success

Principal: Linda Cash
School Counselor(s): Emily Jenkins
Enrollment: 421

Principal's Comment

Mrs. Jenkins is an excellent advocate for family and community involvement. She goes above and beyond her job as a school counselor to assist and involve family members, community members and other stakeholders in the educational process and success of all the students of Westmoreland Elementary School. She collaborates weekly with at-risk families to assure that each child reaches their fullest academic potential!

Critical Data Element (s)

Number of TCAP Proficient students in Reading/Language Arts.

Systemic Changes

1. Parents, students, and teachers became part of the intervention and change of the school climate.
2. Approaches to positively involve parents increased.
3. Volunteer program "Three for Me" was established.
4. A monthly character education newsletter was developed and implemented.
5. Increase in the number of family involvement activities.
6. Families found a medium through which to become active participants in the school.
7. Families felt more comfortable asking questions about student learning and testing.

Stakeholders Involved

Counselor(s): Implemented programs such as "Three for Me" Volunteer Program, Boo Hoo Breakfast, Parenting Classes, Career Day, Monthly Character Newsletters, Character Words on School Marquee, and Grandparents Day Family Photos/Lunch. Served as a parent/staff liaison to ensure that students received a personalized educational experience.
Administrator: Promoted activities to teachers/staff and parents. Supported and helped fund service projects opportunities. Acted as a liaison between teachers/staff and parents.

Faculty/Staff: Began moving from "normal" parties to educational/informative parties, where students perform or teachers "teach" parents literacy skills.
Students: Participated in activities that fostered parental involvement and built character. Actively encouraged families to participate and supported school events and activities.
Parents: Promoted and supported events such as PTO Family Skate Night, Teacher Appreciation Volunteers, Field Trips, Career Day, Multicultural Fair, and Science Fair. Completed climate surveys at the end of the year.
County Agency Members: Gallatin Skate Center and Westmoreland Public Library participated in Career Day.

Results

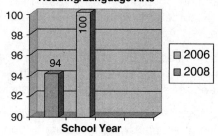

Percentage of Students Proficient in Reading/Language Arts

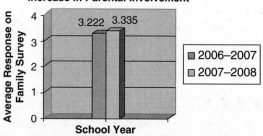

Increase in Parental Involvement

Faces Behind the Data

This MEASURE piece was unlike any piece I have completed thus far. Our goal was to improve families' opinion of the school climate by increasing the number of positive family/school activities thus improving TCAP scores. The Grandparents' Day Luncheon/Family Photos was by far the best addition we made to our school's activity list. Being the photographer for this event gave me the prime opportunity to see the family unit at work. As I stood in the library watching the families enter, dressed in their Sunday best, tending to their hair as well as their spouse's; interacting with their children/grandchildren and simply being "the family," I learned more information about that child's family than in any other event we have ever held. This event reaffirmed the fact that families are not ALWAYS intimidated by the school setting, thus making a paradigm shift from "formal" to "personal" school events, which will decrease families' anxieties in the school setting.

MEASURE

Mission, Element, Analyze, Stakeholders-Unite, Results, Educate
A Six-step Accountability Process for School Counselors

Name and Address of School:
Westside Middle School
3389 Dawn Dr.
Memphis, TN 38127

Principal:
Willie C. Williams

Name of Counselor(s) Leading the Initiative:
Earnestine Benton

Enrollment:
397

School Demographics:
Caucasian/Non-Hispanic: 1.2%
African American: 98.3%
Hispanic: 0.5%
Free Lunches: 98.9%
Reduced Lunches: 143.5%
English as Second Language: 0.8%
Exceptional Student Education/Special Education: 20.2%

STEP ONE: MISSION

MISSION
Connect your work to your school's mission in keeping with the ASCA or your state's comprehensive school counseling model.

Your school or department's mission statement is:
The mission of Westside Middle School is to provide all students with the skills and knowledge needed to become advanced in reading, writing, math, critical thinking, and the use of technology, preparing them for education beyond middle/high school and competence in the future workforce.

STEP TWO: ELEMENT

ELEMENT
What critical data element are you trying to impact? Examples include grades, test scores, attendance, promotion rates, graduation rates, post-secondary going rate, enrollment into honors or AP courses, special education, discipline referral data and so on.
　　What is the baseline for the data element? Where do you hope to move it (goal)?

Element : School-wide discipline referrals, expulsions, suspensions.
Baseline: Discipline Referrals 1724, Expulsions 152, Suspensions 992.
Goal: Decrease school-wide discipline by 50%.

STEP THREE: ANALYZE

ANALYZE THE DATA ELEMENT
You can use percentages, averages, raw scores, quartiles, or stanines. You can aggregate or disaggregate the data to better understand which students are meeting success. You can disaggregate by gender, race, ethnicity, socio-economic status, or in a multitude of ways to look at student groupings.

The Baseline Data revealed:
In the 2007–2008 school year, there were 1,724 discipline referrals, 152 expulsions, and 992 suspensions.

STEP FOUR: STAKEHOLDERS-UNITE

STAKEHOLDERS-UNITE TO DEVELOP STRATEGIES TO IMPACT THE DATA ELEMENT

Beginning Date: August 2008
Ending Date: April 2009

Stakeholders	Strategies
School Counselor(s)	• Delivered faculty and staff training for identification of bullies and overage students. • Notified faculty of bully repeaters. • Conducted S-Teams to decrease bullying. • Implemented a program to remove students who were two or more grades behind from middle school. • Conducted S-Teams for teachers in response to bullying and aggressive behaviors. • Delivered classroom guidance on bullying and conflict resolution. • Conducted problem-solving groups. • Helped establish a peer mediation program. • Worked closely with a community agency to provide sessions for conflict resolution. • Honored students with certificates for acts of kindness.
Administrator(s)	• Provided leadership and support for all facets of the program. • Compared 2007–2008 and 2008–2009 school year data.
Behavioral Specialist	• Enforced consequences. • Worked with staff to improve classroom school climate. • Supported every facet of the discipline plan.
Teachers	• Supported and participated in the S-Teams process. • Collaborated with counselors to create safe classrooms. • Focused on a team approach to assist students rather than writing office referrals. • Implemented behavioral interventions for students.
Students	• Participated in peer mediation and anger management training. • Actively participated in classroom guidance. • Identified bullies and told adults. • Learned when to seek help from adults.
Coaches	• Encouraged students to join sports teams to learn discipline.
Parents	• Attended S-Team meetings to discuss their child's behavior. • Asked counselor for strategies to help their child.
Parent Teacher Associations	• Helped in PTO meetings where the mission of the school was shared. • Welcomed parents to serve as volunteers at the school.
School Psychologists	• Held weekly meetings to support S-Teams and IEPs.
Social Workers	• Provided weekly group and individual counseling sessions for students. • Supported S-Team process.
Living Legacy Agency	• Provided an eight-week program to service students with multiple suspensions and behavioral issues.

Stakeholders	Strategies
Faith-Based Organizations	• Developed a minister's alliance.
Youth and Community Associations	• Girl's Inc. provided trainers for students.
Colleges and Universities	• College interns who were mentored by counselor Benton supported the program.
Classroom Teacher Assistants	• Supported discipline plan consistently.
Other Support Staff (front office, custodial, cafeteria, playground)	• Made counselor aware of actual and potential situations of conflict.
School Improvement Team	• Reviewed data.
Resources (grants, technology, etc.)	• Girls Inc. approved grant to purchase conflict resolution workbooks.

STEP FIVE: RESULTS

RESULTS

Restate your baseline data.
State where your data is now. Did you meet your goal?

Restate baseline data: Results (data now):   Met goal: Yes X No: _____

School Year	2007–2008	2008–2009
Occurrences	1,724	774
Expulsions	152	31
Suspensions	992	237

Questions to Consider as you examine results and revise your MEASURE:

Which strategies had a positive impact on the data?
S-Teams, consistent meetings with parents throughout the year, grade-level team meetings w/teachers, comparison of data w/faculty through COMPSTAT reports, and the extensive involvement of social worker.

Which strategies should be replaced, changed, added?
S-Teams should be held on certain days after the first six weeks. The school social worker had a tremendous impact on the discipline team, but his position has been terminated due to budget woes. We fear we may have serious repercussions when he leaves.

Based on what you have learned, how will you revise Step Four "Stakeholders-Unite?"
We will support Girls' Inc. earlier in the year, since they are now in place.

How did your MEASURE contribute to systemic change(s) in your school and/or in your community?
The number of discipline referrals for 2007–2008 were 1,724 vs. 2008–2009 774 as of April 29.
The number of suspensions for 2007–2008 was 992 vs. 2008–2009 237 as of April 29.
The number of students expelled 2007–2008 was 152 vs. 2008–2009 31 as of April 29.
Promotional Rate and Attendance Improved!

STEP SIX: EDUCATE

Educate others concerning efforts to move data. Develop a report card that shows how the work of the school counselor(s) is connected to the mission of the schools and to student success. Below is an example of a report card.

Westside Middle School MEASURE of Success

Principal: Willie C. Williams
School Counselor: Earnestine Benton
Enrollment: 419

Principal's Comment:

Mrs. Benton takes a leadership role and collaborates so that our students can succeed. As a result of her hard work with the discipline team we have a 55% reduction in office referrals, 80% reduction in expulsions, and 77% reduction in suspensions. Mrs. Benton is an outstanding counselor.

School Counselor(s)'s Comment

Discipline referrals were at an unacceptable level (1724) for entire school year 2007–2008.

Critical Data Element(s)

Reduce discipline referrals for entire school by 50%.

Systemic Changes

A new discipline plan was initiated.

Intervention teams on each grade level are the norm.

Stakeholders are really involved.

The school's approach to office referrals and suspensions has changed. S-Teams are a major part of our discipline plan.

Stakeholders Involved

Counselor(s): Earnestine Benton, Robert Oselen
Administrator: Provided strong leadership and effort for all facets of the program and helped disaggregate data.
Social Worker: Supported the S-Team process and used small groups for issues involving behavioral intervention.
Teachers: Supported classroom guidance.
Behavioral Specialist: Wrote behavioral interventions for Red Zone Students, provided individual counseling about conflict resolution and helped disaggregate data for the discipline team.
Parents: Supported the S-Team meetings.
Students: Learned when to seek help from an adult and were involved in classroom discussions.
Business Partners: The Living Legacy offered an eight week course for conflict resolution and peer mediation. Girls Inc. approved a grant for purchasing publications on peer mediation.

Results

Discipline Referrals: decreased 55%.
Expulsions: decreased 80%
Suspensions: decreased 77%

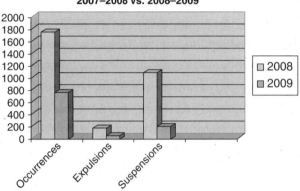

Discipline Comparison
2007–2008 vs. 2008–2009

Faces Behind the Data

Students are more focused academically since we have met our behavioral objectives. Other schools are asking what we did differently. We are proud that we have six students to apply for a middle school college. We had 55 overage students apply for a prep school and get accepted. Other students are now asking to be a part of our more challenging programs within the school and outside the school. We had two students who were having some behavioral issues ask to be placed in honors courses.

Springfield Public Schools An Urban School System

MEET: Yolanda D. Johnson, Director of Student Support Services, and Sonia Dinnall, Acting Supervisor of Student Support Services

> *"We have talked way too long about the value, expertise, professionalism, commitment of school counselors, etc...now let's show them what we have! There is no time better than the present for counselors across this nation to collectively respond to the urgency that we are dealing with in our public school system in the United States. Now is our time to respond to our call to serve by advocating for educational equity for all students, which is the heart of our work. However, we must do so in a manner where counselors share accountability for student outcomes and contribute to moving critical data in a positive direction. It is my belief that we have counselors who will and can respond to the call to serve as leaders to improve student academic success."*
>
> (Yolanda D. Johnson, Director of Student Support Services, Springfield Public Schools)

Our motivation for implementing MEASURE as a pilot in the Springfield Public Schools System began with a vision and belief that counselors are knowledgeable professionals who contribute to student achievement. The results of a needs assessment of comprehensive school counseling programs in Springfield Public Schools during the 2007–2008 school year revealed that there was not only an implementation gap, but counselors did not consistently align their work with school/district improvement goals. Counselors were able to articulate/document their actions (counselor activities/ interventions); however, a key element that was missing was the results of their actions (counselor activities/interventions). The concept of results was a very delicate issue as it could have the implications/perception that counselors were not doing a good job, or counselors were ineffective, and that concept did not align with our vision or beliefs. We knew that we had to realign our practice to get to the heart of the work, which is accountability for student success. As Patricia J. Martin would

say, it is about "deliberate actions, which can be documented by "hard data," moving counseling from the periphery to the front and center." And of course, we believe that counselors should be front and center because they are Masters level professionals who are competent and committed to our children, and who can contribute to the success of our students.

Concurrently, during the needs assessment phase, the district was conducting a national search for a new Superintendent of Schools. As our new superintendent, Dr. Alan J. Ingram, took his place as the leader of the district, he brought a new mission and vision as well as strategic priorities to Springfield. As he studied the data and critical issues of the district, he made improving attendance (along with other critical data elements) one of his strategic priorities. As he stated in his letter to colleagues, "I know we have pockets of success in our schools, but we must move to spread that success system wide, to every school, every classroom." Armed with this statement and with Dr. Ingram's full support, the Director of Student Support Services was highly motivated to pursue the next step in the renaissance of Springfield public school's comprehensive school counseling model. In August 2008, all K–12 counselors were given a workshop on school counselor accountability by Dr. Carol Dahir. It was during that workshop that counselors were provided with training on MEASURE. During one of the small group activities, counselors were told to write down some of the pressing issues at their school, and attendance was the first item listed across all grade levels. That served as the entry point to engage counselors in aligning school counselor practice with the need to make positive changes to a critical data element, using MEASURE in their schools. MEASURE served as a vehicle for counselors to successfully utilize data to inform their best practices. In addition, MEASURE empowered counselors to have a greater voice and to be seen as the leaders that we know they are.

How did you get your counselors to "buy in"? What was their receptivity?

At the conclusion of the workshop provided by Dr. Dahir, counselors were asked to participate in developing a MEASURE to improve student attendance. Additional training was held for all counselors in the district. All principals were provided with an overview and training as well. Ongoing support was also provided.

Counselors bought in once they learned that their principal had been provided with an overview of MEASURE, as it allowed principals and counselors to work collaboratively on the attendance issue. It also helped a great deal to have one of the authors of MEASURE conduct the professional development. This allowed the counselors of the district to fully understand the vision, scope, and effectiveness of a carefully implemented MEASURE. As a result, schools that were receptive decided to participate in the pilot, seventeen schools in all. Many counselors embraced the idea of working collaboratively with their principals to improve student attendance. The level of organization that MEASURE requires helped counselors see the focus it brought to their work. It aligned the work of the counselor with district goals and engendered greater accountability for all district staff.

Each individual counseling department was responsible for sharing their results with their principal on a regular basis. This was done in a manner that was best suited for each school. Some reported results quarterly, some biweekly, and others only at midyear. The principals of the schools who participated in the pilot were extremely pleased with the results. Great gains were achieved in the attendance rate for the targeted populations. Principals found MEASURE to be perfectly aligned to the School Improvement Plan, as well as in full support of student achievement. For example, one elementary school posted an increase of 23.6% in attendance! A principal of one of the pilot middle schools said, "The Counseling Team of M. Marcus Kiley Middle School is an integral and vital component of our Leadership Team; [with their work] grounded in the philosophies and goals articulated in the Massachusetts Model for School Counseling Programs. The goals of the counseling department are clearly aligned with the goals of the current 2008–2009 School Improvement Plan. Improving school attendance is a targeted goal."

In addition, when the revised counseling policy was shared with the principals, MEASURE came up as an example of accountability tools. A middle school counselor and principal had the opportunity to share the positive outcome of their collaboration in helping the district improve student attendance by using MEASURE. There was also an opportunity to share this success with the School Committee. Overall, the reaction was positive as it provided a clear example of how counselors can be contributors to improving student success.

Pilot Participating Schools and Results

School Name	Lead Counselor(s)	# of students	School Improvement Goal	Results
Forest Park Middle School	Margaret Wynne	890	Increase attendance rate for all students	07–08 08–09 MP1 90.5% 95.0% MP2 89.4% 96.5% MP3 89.6% 94.6% MP4 89.4% 91.2%
Frank H. Freedman Elementary School	Deirdre Stancil	297	Increase attendance rate of Hispanic students by 25%	07–08 08–09 68.2% 92.6% (24.4% increase)
M. Marcus Kiley Middle School	Dawna Jenne, James Goodwin, Nancy Giza	829	Increase by 2% attendance for 7th & 8th grade at-risk students	07–08 08–09 67% 87% (20% increase)
Science Technology Engineering and Math Middle School (STEM)	Tracy Sasanecki	100	Increase math grades (GPA) of 27 at-risk students by 25%	The math grades (GPA) of 7 students were increased. This represents a 25.9% increase.

Rutherford County Schools, Tennessee
A Suburban School System

MEET: Leigh Bagwell & Karen Meador, Student Services Counselor Liaisons

When our district began the process of developing a comprehensive school counseling program, we felt that it would be important to address the accountability component. Who best to direct how we are held accountable than the counselors ourselves? A small group of counselors served as the steering committee for our entire initiative. These brave folks were willing to be leaders in our district, as well as the state, and began piloting MEASURE in August of 2007. As the district counselor liaisons we felt that it was important to lead by example. We also wanted to show the effectiveness of our district programs by positively impacting the critical data elements for which the school system is held accountable.

The steering committee quickly identified that unless counselors could demonstrate their accountability, the district might place more significance on fulfilling non-counseling responsibilities. The counselors wanted to show how their specific talents could affect children academically, emotionally, socially and in the development of future career plans. MEASURE would give them an opportunity to show how what they do makes a difference in those critical areas for schools, such as discipline, attendance, and academic achievement. While our counselors weren't excited about additional paper work, essentially doing "something else," they all learned how to incorporate MEASURE into their current programs. It took district leadership examples and additional experience but now they all see how it can be an excellent tool to demonstrate their value as school counselors.

We have had the opportunity to share the impact of the school counselors with the Board of Education, and we were thrilled to be able to highlight the district counselors who were recognized by the State

Pilot Participating Schools and Results

School Name School Year	Lead Counselor(s)	# of students	School Improvement Goal	Results
Cedar Grove Elementary 2007–2008	Sherrye Teague	951	Increase Parental Involvement of at-risk students by 10%	Parental Involvement increased for: 52.4% identified at-risk K students. 27.8% identified at-risk 1st graders. 31.3% identified at-risk 2nd graders.
LaVergne Lake Elementary 2008–2009	Laura Deer	911	Increase 5th Grade Writing Assessment scores by one or more points for 85% of program participants	92% of the students participating in the program increased their writing assessment score by at least 1 point. 31% of the students participating in the program increased their writing assessment score by 2 or more points.
LaVergne High School 2007–2008	Stacie Frazier & Steven Lay	2001	Increase 9th grade promotion rate of identified at-risk students by 10%	71.4% of the original 56 9th graders identified at-risk of failure were promoted to the 10th grade.
LaVergne High School 2008–2009	Stacie Frazier, Steven Lay, Scherrie Anderson	2016	Increase 9th grade promotion rate of identified at-risk students by 10%	69% of the original 70 9th graders identified at-risk of failure were promoted to the 10th grade.
Riverdale High School 2008–2009	Bentley Shofner	2165	Reduce failure rate of incoming 9th grade students by 1%	The freshman failure rate at the end of the 2007–2008 school year was 8%. At the end of the 2008–2009 school year the freshman failure rate was 6%. That is a 2% decrease.
Siegel Middle School 2007–2008	Tommie Barrett & Daniel Gregory	1062	Increase the number of students staying on Principal's List and/or Honor Roll all year by 10%	At the end of the year 248 students remained on principal's list and/or honor roll all six weeks. In the previous year, only 41 students earned principal's list for the entire year.
Stewartsboro Elementary 2008–2009	Shannon Ritchie & Marsha Thompson	1188	Reduce administrative discipline referrals for student behavior by 10%	The number of discipline referrals for student behavior went from 438 to 366. That is a 16% decrease.
Student Services Department 2007–2008	Leigh Bagwell & Karen Meador	36,500	Increase the graduation rate by 1%	Graduation rate for 2007 was 87.5%. Graduation rate for 2008 was 88.0%. The district saw a .5% increase in the graduation rate.
Student Services Department 2008–2009	Leigh Bagwell & Karen Meador	36,700	Increase referrals to Student Assistance Teams by 20%	The number of SAT referrals increased from 47 to 711. Last year there were 62 Section 504 referrals. That was increased to 212 this year.

Department of Education for their work with MEA-SURE. Counselors have shared outcomes with their principals and gotten a lot of positive feedback. Principals have encouraged their counselors to continue to lead these sorts of initiatives.

Salem-Keizer Public Schools, Oregon A Suburban School System

MEET: Marilyn Rengert and Marnie Grimell, Program Associates, Counseling Department, Student Services

When Salem-Keizer district was selected by the Oregon Department of Education to undertake the implementation of the new Oregon Comprehensive Guidance and Counseling Framework in 2004, we faced the daunting task of transforming a large district's philosophy, practice and culture around school counseling. Many staff had been in the district for 15+ years. Many came from mental health, community, career counseling, and social work backgrounds. While we shared a common vision for helping to support student success, we lacked a common language, consistent practice, and accountability.

After four years of "storming, forming, norming and performing," the implementation Steering Committee was confident that the counseling staff (104 counselors in K–12 schools) was ready to use the MEASURE as a next major step in demonstrating accountability. In the fall of 2008, a staff in-service was held to introduce the MEASURE, with process guidelines. Each staff member was required to identify site-based needs from student data and submit an Advocacy Plan (our internal name for the MEASURE). They had the year to implement, evaluate and submit their plans. MEASURE is now an annual requirement for all counseling staff.

Critical to our success was involving each and every one of our principals. Each counselor had to evaluate the student outcome data for their MEASURE Advocacy Plan, and **discuss** the results with their principal. Principals were asked to write comments and sign the plan for submission to Student Services. Additionally, the Program Associates and Counseling Coordinator presented exemplary MEASURES to middle and high school principals during the 2008 and 2009 school years. Principals were most enthusiastic when the counseling outcome data correlated

A Sample of Participating Schools and Results

School Name	Lead Counselor(s)	# of students	School Improvement Goal	Results
Brush College Elementary	Patty Parvin	421	Increase state test scores for 4th and 5th graders	Increased 5th grade reading–28%, 5th grade math–34%, 4th grade reading–31%, 4th grade math–49%.
Candalaria Elementary	Rene Manley	310	Increase reading scores in 3–5th graders	85% of target group met state reading benchmark.
Grant Elementary	Aaron Bremiller	447	Improve attendance in students not meeting math state benchmarks	44% of target group improved attendance by at least 10%.
Hammond Elementary	Heather Moon	515	Increase number of students' service-learning hours	Nearly doubled hours spent by students in service learning activities.
Houck Middle School	Cheryl Marion, Stephen Moe	971	Increase attendance for 6th graders	Increased attendance by 2.95%.
Middle Grove Elementary	Kari Lamont	251	Decrease discipline referrals school wide	Decreased total referrals by 58%.
Lamb Elementary	Ruth Larson	502	Improve reading level for 1st graders	Target group moved from 0 reading level to average of level 8.
Schirle Elementary	Coleen VanDreal	460	Reduce number of aggression referrals	16% reduction in aggression referrals.
Swegle Elementary	Jen Loganbill	530	Improve student rating in Characteristics of Successful Learner	47% improved from Needs Improvement.
Judson Middle School	Gloria Flager	948	Reduce number of Fs	15% reduction in number of Fs.
Parrish Middle School	Cathy Taylor, Bill Hawkins	639	Increase attendance	Improved attendance by 2.5%.
South Salem High School	Sherri Buck	1881	Decrease dropout rate	Decreased dropout rate by 3%.

with academic, attendance, and behavioral improvement and dovetailed with the goals on their comprehensive school improvement plans. Principals said they would be more actively involved in the process of helping their counselors write MEASURE Advocacy Plans for the next school year. Principals also were more supportive of removing non-counseling duties from their counseling staff, to give them more time to focus on data driven plans related to school improvement goals.

With a staff of 100+, we are still encouraging just a handful of counselors and their principals to comply with our Comprehensive Guidance and Counseling requirements, including the MEASURE.

Now in our fifth year of implementation, Salem-Keizer Public Schools Counseling Department is recognized throughout Oregon as a leader in school counseling. Counseling staff have become integral members of their site councils and district advisory committees. We have seen school counseling grow up and grow into the highly respected profession we knew it could be. Oregon's Comprehensive Guidance and Counseling Framework, and the easy-to-use and understand MEASURE, provided us with clear guidelines to an accountability process, and a map that we will follow as we continue this exciting and challenging journey. We are excited about shaping the very bright future of school counseling.

Connecticut Technical High School System A Statewide System for Career and Technical Education

MEET: Kim Traverso, Central Office Education Consultant

To demonstrate the effectiveness of the Connecticut Technical High School System's school counseling program, staff and their stakeholders use data. It helps them document how they have an impact on student academic achievement and success, as well as the impact of the program on the goals of NCLB. Data can be used to document the results of classroom lessons, the individual student planning sessions by grade level, and the strategies and interventions used to improve student academic achievement and equitable access for all students to programs and resources (State of Connecticut State Board of Education, 2008).

Data informs, confirms progress and reveals shortcomings in student performance (Stone & Dahir, 2006). CTHSS school counseling departments have designed and implemented, in all 17 schools, a MEASURE based on the Connecticut Comprehensive School Counseling Program's self-study guide. Each school collects and analyzes student data to inform and guide the development of a comprehensive school counseling program based on school-wide issues. A few examples of the critical data elements targeted this year are: bullying, attendance, honors, retention and graduation rates. Each school included all stakeholders in the process and set up a systematic approach in follow-up, reflection, and monitoring progression, and they made sure to make the necessary adjustments, analyzing data and evaluating outcomes. This process has made their school counseling departments more cohesive and collaborative with school building and community stakeholders so that informed decisions could be made about how to improve student outcomes.

The use of data is the key to demonstrating the effectiveness of the school counseling program and to developing practices that can lead to higher levels of success. Using data enables school counselors to work in tandem with building administrators and faculty to close the achievement gap. School

School Name	Lead Counselor(s)	# of students	School Improvement Goal	Results
Brush College Elementary	Patty Parvin	421	Increase state test scores for 4th and 5th graders.	Increased 5th grade reading–28%, 5th grade math–34%, 4th grade reading–31%, 4th grade math–49%.
Platt Technical High School	Mazzonna, Arestia, Farley, Mihalik, Wade, Galarraga, Heller	912	Increase student involvement in activities and school/community volunteerism.	147 additional students participated in other clubs and school wide activities during the year.
Henry Abbott Technical High School	Isabel Sweeney, Molly LeFort, Samantha Palma, Shannon Feeley	577	Maintain 9th grade retention rate at 96%.	Ninth grade retention rate is currently at 94%.
E.C. Goodwin Technical High School	Ericka Shevchenko, Brian Pereira, Ed Heath	481	Increase core subject grade average by 5 points for 70% of students in the group.	50% of the students increased their average; only 20% students increased their average by 5% points.

counselors can collaborate with faculty to devise strategies that will enable more students to move successfully from grade level to grade level. When school counselors work with the same school-based data as their colleagues, they share accountability for student outcomes and contribute to moving critical data elements in a positive direction (State of Connecticut State Board of Education, 2008).

Rochester City School District
An Urban School System

MEET: Dr. Bonnie J. Rubenstein, Director of School Counseling,

In 2003, the Rochester City School District school counselors stepped up their commitment to implement the New York State School Counselor Association Comprehensive School Counseling Model of which accountability and MEASURE are important components.

The model and MEASURE truly helped us turn a corner and establish school counselors as contributors to student achievement. Prior to 2003, cuts to school counseling positions were threatened every budget season. Since that time, counselors and educational leaders have worked tirelessly to collaborate to obtain and use data showing the impact of school counseling programs on the academic achievement of students. These efforts have been successful, resulting in a dramatic increase in school counseling positions from 56 to 90 counselors across our district.

Counselors bought in because of a grass roots effort by a small group of counselors themselves with support from their Central Office Director. The East High School counselors developed a comprehensive school counseling pilot in 2003–2004, and school counselor leader Christine Frederick from East High School presented their completed MEASURE to all counselors at a citywide meeting during the 2004–2005 school year. Since 2005, Rochester City School District counselors have made presentations to the superintendent and central office leaders numerous times and, most recently, to 120 school administrators (including principals, and district wide and central office directors) during spring 2008. During the 2009 school year, a summary of the results of the impact of their work was shared with the superintendent and school board. In these stressful economic times, school counseling was one of the only departments not experiencing any staff reductions and in actuality, counselors were added to four secondary buildings.

With almost 15,000 students in our system, our goal was to increase the graduation rate district wide. In order to model this initiative for the 90 secondary counselors, I undertook this challenge as a district-wide MEASURE initiative. The critical data element was as follows: the percentage of students who graduate four years after entering the grade 9 in fall 2006 cohort.

Results:

2005	2006	2007	2008	2009
41%	39%	48%	54%	AUG. 22

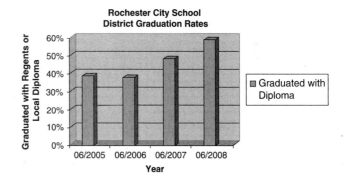

Rochester City School District Graduation Rates

Additionally, five high schools exceeded the state benchmark of 55% in August 2008: School of the Arts 88%, Wilson Magnet High School 68%, Bioscience and Health Careers at Franklin 65%, Charlotte High School 58%, and Marshall High School 58%. With East High leading the way in 2006 with our first MEASURE, our high schools now understand the importance of utilizing data to better understand who is succeeding and who is not.

We must continue to press on in our efforts to implement school counseling programs that are proactive, data-driven, and developmentally appropriate. Our students deserve school counselors who are leaders and agents of systemic change and work tirelessly as their advocates.

CHAPTER 6

Preparing Graduate Students to Be Data-Driven Practitioners

MEASURE is not only an excellent strategy for putting accountability into perspective for school counselors, but it has given me a structure for helping graduate students understand the connection between the school counseling program, the mission of the school, and counselor contributions to student success."

Patricia A. Landers, School Counseling Adjunct,
Central Connecticut State University

This next generation of school counselors is in a pivotal position to help students wed academic rigor with affective development, and thus help close the information, opportunity, and achievement gaps. Across the United States, efforts are underway to prepare data informed school counselors who, through words, behaviors, and actions, will contribute to improving student achievement by designing and delivering student strategies and interventions that support, prevent and motivate.

From the introductory course in school counseling, through courses in research and special needs learning, to the culminating experience of internship, MEASURE has proven to be an effective tool for integrating data-informed practice into the curriculum. What follows are sample assignments from counselor educators who utilize MEASURE to teach and reinforce the alignment of social justice and data-informed practice.

ACTION RESEARCH AND SCHOOL COUNSELOR ACCOUNTABILITY

Action research requires the use of data-informed practice and follows the scientific method of inquiry, including developing a hypothesis, gathering data, analyzing and interpreting data, and then applying the results to improve practice (Lewin, 1946; Mills, 2003; Sagor, 2005). Classroom teachers (school counselors) who conduct such research are "reflective practitioners" and can make exemplary contributions to school improvement (Suter, 2006). Lewis (1981) reminded us, "No research without action. No action without research" (as cited in Minor, 1981, p. 485).

MEASURE provides students with a clear framework and method for understanding the work of school counselors. After courses in theory, skills, ethics, and research methods, MEASURE is an effective tool for demonstrating how previous learning comes together in professional practice. MEASURE provides students with a clear working knowledge of data-driven decision-making, action research, collaboration, evidence-based practices, and program evaluation. MEASURE also helps students transfer from the micro level to the macro level. In other words, students transfer their understanding of MEASURE as a process for addressing a single need or creating a single intervention, to the larger programmatic structure of a school counseling program.

(Erin Mason, Assistant Professor De Paul University)

With a growing demand for outcome-based evidence coupled with the increased pressures of accountability (Isaacs, 2003; Bauman, 2004; Brown & Trusty, 2005), action research serves as an important vehicle for school counseling practitioners to articulate their contributions to student achievement. Thus, action research offers school counselors a tool to act, progress, and reform, rather than simply accept stability and mediocrity (Marzano, 2003; Mills, 2003).

MEASURE offers a systematic way for school counselors to explore a school-based problem, develop a possible course of action, and monitor progress and results. Action research is collaborative, realistic, and empowers participants (Rowell, 2006). When school counselors use a mixed-methodology, action research approach, they are able to contribute to the goals of school improvement.

School personnel nationwide face enormous challenges in providing every student with an education that ensures every student will graduate with options after high school, including college (ASCA, 1997; 2003; 2005). Action research can provide evidence that school counselors can initiate, develop, lead, and coordinate programs that contribute to systemic change and improved learning success for every student.

Counselor Educators Teaching with MEASURE

MEASURE was written primarily with the practicing school counselor in mind, but what the authors quickly discovered after the first edition was published is that MEASURE was being used as a valuable tool for many school counselor educators to prepare their school counseling candidates for the challenges of working in schools. Reports from counselor educators, such as those featured in this chapter and the referenced authors' work with school counseling candidates, reveals five major themes: 1) School District In-service Programs; 2) Introductory School Counseling Courses; 3) Research Courses; 4) School Counselors and Special Needs Students Courses; and 5) Practica and Internship Courses.

School District In-services. Counselor educators are providing data in-services to local, state and national school districts, helping practicing school counselors, as Joy Burnham of the University of Alabama puts it, "with their conceptualization and design of MEASUREs at their schools" (personal communication, December 15, 2009). Ellen Slicker, Professor at Middle Tennessee State University, talks

about planting the seeds by helping districts "take over their own MEASURE training and moving ahead" (personal communication, December 10, 2009).

Counselor Educators are fostering collaborative relationships with school districts whose district-level, Supervisors of Guidance and Counseling are under pressure to bring school counselors into data-driven practice. By going in and helping practicing school counselors become comfortable with data use through a simple six-step framework, they are furthering a working relationship with the district supervisors and school counselors. "MEASURE is a great vehicle for instigating collaborative relationships with school counselors in the field" (J. Burnham, personal communication, December 15, 2009).

MEASURE in-service programs, delivered by counselor educators, are especially helpful in creating a situation where graduates can practice assuming a leadership role in the use of data with fewer obstacles. Candidates can learn how to use data, without being thwarted nay sayers, as more and more systems are moving in a data-driven direction.

Introductory School Counseling Courses. MEASURE is often used in beginning courses in order to familiarize school counseling candidates with their need to be part of the accountability imperative. Courses such as "The Organization and Administration of School Counseling," "Counseling in the Schools," or "Introduction to the School Counseling Profession," often include the first four steps of MEASURE as a non-threatening way of introducing data work to school counseling candidates. This includes, when possible, having the candidates go into a school and practice discussing their accountability MEASURE project with practicing counselors. It is during this early hands-on experience that the candidate will retrieve actual student data.

"I found that bringing our school counselors-in-training into the schools early-on in their training (i.e., prior to practica, internship) is invaluable. By utilizing the MEASURE—an attractive way for our school counseling students to offer something useful and worthwhile to busy counselors—it is easy for our school counselors-in-training to get into the schools for important initial clinical experiences" (J. Burnham, personal communication, December 15, 2009).

Hattie Isen of Cambridge College delivers MEASURE training in the introductory course "Counseling in the Schools." MEASURE generates "conversations around challenging events or problems with real and appropriate data sources" (H. Isen, personal communication, December 8, 2009). MEASURE examines the education issues in America in the context of how school counselors can offer assistance with demonstrable results. Isen uses small community study groups in which her students interact with others to identify possible ways of using a data piece to create an action plan, a MEASURE.

Candidates work solo, or in groups, with a set of data and complete the steps: Mission, Element, Analyze, Stakeholders-Unite. Real data is often not difficult to obtain as usually one group member is a practicing teacher or has an inroad into a school. Names and other identifying information is not included. The first three steps can be completed with real information, but the fourth step, Stakeholders-Unite, is a hypothetical exercise as the students are not really in the school to implement strategies. Sometimes instructors have the students practice the last two steps, Results and Educate, by using hypothetical information, so they practice completing the Results and the Educate part of the MEASURE.

Practicing an accountability project, such as MEASURE, early in the program helps candidates understand that contributing to the academic achievement of students through the use of data is not an add on approach but basic behavior for all 21st-century practicing school counselors (Sink & Stroh, 2003; Cook & Kaffenberger, 2003).

An excerpt from an introductory course syllabus is provided as an example of an introductory course assignment.

SYLLABUS EXCERPT: MEASURE ASSIGNMENT CACREP CORE OBJECTIVES

Research and Program Evaluation

a. The importance of research in advancing the counseling profession.
b. Research methods such as qualitative, quantitative, single-case designs, action research, and outcome-based research.
c. Statistical methods used in conducting research and program evaluation.
d. Principles, models, and applications of needs assessment, program evaluation, and use of findings to effect program modifications.
e. Use of research to inform evidence-based practice
f. Ethical and culturally relevant strategies for interpreting and reporting the results of research and/or program evaluation studies.

CACREP 2009 School Counseling Specialty Areas

Research and Evaluation

Knowledge

a. Understands how to critically evaluate research relevant to the practice of school counseling.
b. Knows current methods of using data to inform decision making and accountability (e.g., school improvement plan, school report card).
c. Understands the outcome research data and best practices as identified in the school counseling research literature.

Skills/Practices

a. Applies relevant research findings to inform the practice of school counseling.

b. Develops measurable outcomes for school counseling programs, activities, interventions, and experiences.
c. Analyzes and uses data to enhance school counseling programs.

Academic Development

Knowledge

a. Understands relationship of the school counseling program to the academic mission of the school.
b. Understands the concepts, principles, strategies, programs and practices that are designed to close the achievement gap and promote students' academic success, and prevent students from dropping out of school.

Skills/Practices

a. Conducts programs that are designed to enhance all students' academic development.

Rubric Point Value

9–10 points

The steps to creating a MEASURE were followed through at least Step 4, and an informative power point presentation was made. The strategies were appropriate for the data, and at least three solid stakeholders with appropriate strategies for their position were identified. The analysis of data was disaggregated to include at least two subsets of data, such as by grade level, ethnicity, gender, or teacher assignment.

5–8 points

The steps to creating a MEASURE were followed through at least Step 4, and an informative PowerPoint presentation was made. The strategies were adequate for the data, and at least three solid stakeholders with adequate strategies for their position were identified. The analysis of data was disaggregated to include at least one subset of data, such as by grade level, ethnicity, gender, or teacher assignment.

0 to 4 points

The steps to creating a MEASURE were inadequate, and the PowerPoint presentation was weak. The strategies were inadequate for the data, and insufficient stakeholders were identified. The analysis of data was inadequate. A meeting between professor and student will be needed if you fail to earn at least a 5 on this assignment.

Your instructions are to develop a MEASURE. Collect real data from a school (we will help you if you have difficulty completing this step). Analyze the data, being vigilant as to the protection of confidentiality. Refer to the guidelines on confidentiality. The analysis should provide insight into any barriers im-

pacting academic achievement for ALL or MANY of the students. Report your findings to the class in a power point presentation. Walk us through the first three steps of MEASURE by mid term.

At the end of the semester, give us a report on your theoretical strategies and stakeholders (Step 4). We know you will not be able to implement any of these strategies during this term but you will complete a MEASURE during the last semester of your last internship. For now, we will do hypothetical work for Step 4 the Stakeholders-Unite step. This final report should be done with a PowerPoint presentation of approximately 10 minutes. Bring copies of Step 4 of your MEASURE (Stakeholders-Unite) for your classmates.

One of the strategies must include developing and delivering a classroom guidance lesson based on school data that demonstrates and models the use of higher-order thinking abilities.

3. **Research Course**   Research can strike fear into the hearts of many graduate students. Action research offers school counselors an opportunity to act, progress, and reform, rather than accept stability and mediocrity (Marzano, 2003; Mills, 2003). Defined as systematic inquiry, action research is conducted by teachers, administrators, counselors, or others with a vested interest in the teaching and learning processes for the purpose of gathering data about how their particular schools operate, how faculty teach, and how students learn (Mills, 2003).

> *I have found that MEASURE provides my students with a cognitive organizer that helps develop accountability procedures. The MEASURE framework gives students a tool to take raw data, describe it, and disaggregate it with an aim towards planning interventions and accountability tools. As these counseling students enter the workforce, they are equipped with a 21st-century accountability structure, which will enhance achievement for all students.*
>
> *(Robert Rotunda, Ed.D., Adjunct Assistant Professor at New York Institute of Technology, NYSSCA President, and Chair of Guidance, Stimson Middle School, Huntington Station, New York)*

When counselor educators teach school counseling candidates the steps to action research they are providing them with a means to answer the question,

"How are students better off academically because they have a school counselor in the school"? Understanding action research also helps school counselors evaluate the effectiveness of their interventions on student achievement and school improvement goals.

4. **School Counselors and Special Needs Students** School counselors serving as consultants to teachers regarding appropriate interventions has been a hallmark of the counseling profession. Newly added in the last decade is the practice of occasionally identifying a particular student's report card data element to improve. For example, if the counselor suggests a behavior management program to reduce a student's discipline incidents, it becomes a data-driven consulting process. Counselor educators describe helping their students check the effectiveness of their interventions through the MEASURE process. "MEASURE demonstrates the power of data-driven strategies, thus prompting our students to move rapidly from envisioning how they can devise an intervention for the targeted problem, to showing the effectiveness of their interventions in measureable terms" (J. Burnham, personal communication, December 15, 2009).

MEASUREs give counselors an easy way to show how counseling interventions and prevention activities can have a direct and positive impact on school improvement goals. They are also a non-threatening way to introduce data collection into the busy

SYLLABUS EXCERPT: MEASURE ASSIGNMENT

Review of school report card/agency annual report data

a. Look up the most recent report card that you can download for the school district in which you live.

b. Review the overall district profile and select one building's data to examine. As a counselor in that building, what is the data telling you about school improvement needs? Choose a data point (one data element) that you think a counseling program can influence.

c. Using the MEASURE template, create a MEASURE action research plan to influence the data point you have chosen, one that will answer the question, "How are students succeeding because of the school counseling program?"

d. Fully complete MEASURE steps 1 through 4

Learner Objective: Demonstrate the ability to apply action research skills in counseling and school settings to improve school and student performance. This assignment is aligned with CACREP 2009 Core 8 e and School Counseling Core J 1,2,3.

---

worlds of school counselors (*Dr. Andrew Finch, Assistant Professor, School Counseling Coordinator, Vanderbilt University*).

5. **Practica and Internship Courses.** In practicum and internship school counseling, candidates actually complete a six-step MEASURE using real data and reporting their results to their classmates, and often also to the members of the school community. "Ellen Slicker describes the process, "Our interns are instructed to use real data (school "report card") for the school where they are interning. By the time our students have created a MEASURE at the beginning of our Program (in Organization and Administration of School Counseling) and then again in both internships, they are well aware of its value to the school."

The internship is often the culminating experience in which all the skill training comes together in demonstration and implementation of these skills. "School counseling interns are learning from the MEASURE that they are leaders and facilitators of school improvement, but they are not solely responsible for all the changes that need to occur. The MEASURE demonstrates school improvement as a joint venture among those in the school and the community (J. Burnham, personal communication, December 15, 2009). My internship students have learned from the MEASURE that school counselors need to be accountable for their contributions with

evidence-based outcomes. MEASURE is the first opportunity for the school counselors-in-training to work closely with school counselors in collaboration to create a MEASURE" (J. Burnham, personal communication, December 15, 2009).

> *MEASURE instills confidence in interns that they can indeed make a difference.*
>
> *MEASURE provides a very useful accountability process for graduate students to learn to use during their practicum/internship placements in collaboration with counselors. They learn to use data to benefit their program and the students they serve.*
>
> (Dr. Roselind Bogner, Associate Professor, School Counseling Coordinator, Niagra University)

Kim Hegg, intern at Central Connecticut State University, used the MEASURE book for the Supervised School Counseling Internship class with Pat Landers, Counselor Educator. Kim describes her internship experience with data use as being able to "prove that children are different as a result of having worked with us. School counselors work very hard to remove barriers to learning, and the MEASURE process is one way to show others the positive impact we are having on students" (K. Hegg, personal communication, November 10, 2009).

The MEASURE assignment leads to secondary gains that are vital (e.g., understanding the school environment, working with school counseling professionals, dealing with actual school problems, becoming team players, and building confidence as school coun-

selors). With MEASURE success, the students observe how they can contribute successfully and can make a difference with children and adolescents" (J. Burnham, personal communication, December 15, 2009).

> *What makes our students marketable in this economy is to make sure you can show effectiveness. That's what superintendent's want when they hire new school counselors.*
>
> (Dr. Patricia W. De Barbieri,Chair, Department of Counseling and School Psychology Southern Connecticut State University)

Below is a table of MEASURE projects implemented by school counseling interns in their school sites.

Using data provides a solid foundation for school counselors to act on their belief system, and to identify and rectify issues that impact every student's ability to achieve at expected levels (Stone & Dahir, 2007). By their willingness to work within an accountability framework, school counselors defy the pervasive belief that socio-economic status and color determine a young person's ability to learn. Accepting this challenge propels school counselors

to accept responsibility as social justice advocates, as well as to focus strategic and intentional interventions on removing barriers to learning, and raising the level of expectations for students from whom little is expected. When school counselors contribute to school improvement goals, they perceive critically, explore widely, and examine their ideas against explicit and considered moral values and empirical data (Learning Point Associates, 2004). School counselors are concerned not only with what learners need to do, but also what they can become, i.e., compassionate, critical thinkers and contributors to society (Partnership for 21st-Century Skills, 2007).

As more and more MEASURE accountability action plans are implemented across the nation, ongoing data collection and analyses will demonstrate the essential role of the school counselor in the school improvement movement. Thus, the use of data-informed practice, MEASURE and action research by school counselor can close the information, opportunity, and achievement gaps.

School Name School Year University Name	Intern	# of Students	School Improvement Goal	Results
New Milford High School 2008–2009 Southern Connecticut State University	Rachel Andersen	1521	Increase students' overall averages by 5 points, and decrease failures by 10%.	42% of the student increased their overall averages by 5 points or more.
PACE High School 2008–2009 Cambridge College	Brenda Watson	800	Increase the number of 12th grade students who access postsecondary education by 20% by May 2009.	90% of 12th grade students accessing postsecondary education opportunities in May 2009, 20% increase from May 2008.
Scholar High School 2008–2009 Cambridge College	Kathy Green	982	Increase the proficiency rate from 68% to 79%.	Data moved from 68% to above the targeted rate of 79% to 81%.
Conte/West Hills Magnet School 2008–2009 (February 6–April 16, 2009) Southern Connecticut State University	Renee Bacon	621	Reduce the number of behavior card changes by 10%.	Total behavior interventions dropped from the baseline of 70 to 63 after intervention. The goal of 10% decrease in overall behavior card changes was achieved.
Nolensville Elementary School 2008–2009 (February–May 2009) Middle Tennessee State University	Katie Carlson	559	Decrease discipline referrals by 6 percent each month for the remainder of the school year.	Discipline referrals decreased from 18 to 13, from February to May.

School Name School Year University Name	Intern	# of Students	School Improvement Goal	Results
Mt. Juliet Elementary School 2008–2009 (March–May 2009) Middle Tennessee State University	Angela Gagen	993	Increase proficiency and advanced Math scores for African Americans to 80% by May 31, 2009.	80.8% of African American students are proficient or advanced with scores in Math.
Simply Educate High School 2008–2009 (August 15, 2008- May 16, 2009) Cambridge College	Marcia Adair	941	Reduce the number of dropouts by 30% and increase the promotion rate by 30% by May 16, 2009.	The attendance rate decreased 21% and the promotion rate increased 10%. The goal was not reached, but there was progress.
J. F. Wahl Elementary School 2008–2009 Cambridge College	Monica Davis	450	Increase the daily school attendance rate by 5% by May 2009.	The strategies and goals were met and exceeded by 2%.
West Side Elementary School 2008–2009 Cambridge College	Tonya Jones	456	Increase the percent of third graders scoring proficient or advanced on the 2009 literacy exam by at least 15%.	The spring 2009 ACTAAP results showed that 61% of third grade students scored proficient or advanced in literacy. The goal was met and exceeded by 3%.
Daniel Hand High School 2007–2008 (September 15- November 13, 2007) Southern Connecticut State University	Melissa McClellan	1240	Increase school attendance for the first trimester for the current school year and therefore improve overall grades.	At the conclusion of the first trimester, 40 students (42%) had improved their attendance, as well as their no longer having a D or F on their report card.
Oxford High School 2008–2009 (February–April 2009) Southern Connecticut State University	Christine Parmelee and Allison Moreira	419	Increase the overall averages (core subjects only) of the students participating in the Academic Skill Building Group by 10% by the end of the third marking period.	9 of the 13 (69%) students increased their overall averages by the end of the third marking period.
Law and Government Academy at Hartford Public High School 2008–2009 (March 3–April 23, 2009) Central Connecticut State University	Colman Long	350	Decrease daily tardiness rate by 10%.	Decreased tardiness rate by 11.1%.

I have been pleased with how quickly our students grasp the notion that leadership, with respect to collecting and analyzing data, will stand them in good stead as novice counselors. They quickly became interested in what the school report cards

revealed and this spurred a focus on both achievement and general diversity issues in schools.

(Dr. Karen Mackie, Assistant Professor, Counselor Education, Warner School of Education, University of Rochester)

REFERENCES

American School Counselor Association. (1997). *The national standards for school counseling programs.* Alexandria, VA: Author.

American School Counselor Association (2003). *The ASCA national model: A framework for school counseling programs.* Washington, D.C.: Author.

American School Counselor Association. (2005). *American school counselor association national model: A framework for school counseling programs* (2nd ed.). Alexandria, VA: Author.

Bauman, S. (2004). School counselors and research revisited. *Professional School Counseling, 7*(3), 141–151.

Brown, D. & Trusty, J. (2005). The ASCA National Model, accountability, and establishing causal links between school counselors' activities and student outcomes: A reply to Sink. *Professional School Counseling, 9,* 13–15.

Cook, J.B., & Kaffenberger, C.J. (2003). Solution shop: A solution-focused counseling and study skills program for middle school. *Professional School Counseling, 7*(2), 116–123.

Isaacs, M.L. (2003). Data-driven decision-making: The engine of accountability. *Professional School Counseling, 6*(4), 288–295.

Learning Point Associates. (2004). *All students reaching the top: Strategies for closing academic achievement gaps.* Naperville, IL: North Central Regional Education Laboratory.

Lewin, K. (1946). Action research and minority problems. *Journal of Social Issues, 2,* 34–46.

Marzano, R. (2003). *What works in schools, translating research into action.* Alexandria, VA: Association for Supervision and Curriculum Development.

Mills, G.E. (2003). *Action research: A guide for the teacher researcher* (2nd ed.). Upper Saddle River, NJ: Merrill

Minor, B.J. (1981). Bridging the gap between research and practice: An introduction. *Personnel & Guidance Journal, 59,* 485–487.

Partnership for 21st-Century Skills. (2007). *Framework for 21st-century learning.* Tuscan, AZ: Author.

Rowell, L. (2006). Action research and school counseling: Closing the gap between research and practice. *Professional School Counseling, 9*(5), 376–384.

Sagor, R. (2005). *The action research guidebook: A four-step process for educators and school teams.* Thousand Oaks, CA: Corwin Press, Inc.

Sink, C. A., & Stroh, H. R. (2003). Raising achievement test scores of early elementary School students through comprehensive school counseling programs. *Professional School Counseling, 6*(5), 350–365.

Stone, C., & Dahir, C. (2007). *School counselor accountability: A measure of student success* (2nd ed.). Columbus, OH: Merrill Prentice-Hall.

Suter, W. N. (2006). *Introduction to educational research: A critical thinking approach.* Thousand Oaks, CA: Sage.

Appendix A

Participants in the 2001 Education Trust Accountability Meetings

Anderson, Laurel
Past Supervisor of Guidance Services
Duval County Public Schools
Jacksonville, FL

Anderson, Ron
Senior Director of Guidance and Social Work
Wake County Public Schools
Raleigh, NC

Colbert, Robert
Associate Professor
University of Massachusetts
Amherst, MA

Dahir, Carol
Assistant Professor
New York Institute of Technology
Old Westbury, New York

Gysbers, Norm
Professor
University of Missouri
Columbia, Missouri

House, Reese
Principal Investigator
The Education Trust
Washington, DC

Jackson, Greg
Assistant Professor
California State University, Northridge
Northridge, CA

Johnson, Curly
Professional Update
San Juan Capistrano, CA

Kaye, Dawn
State Department of Education
Salt Lake City, Utah

Lockhart, Trish
Director of Guidance
Palmdale High School
Palmdale, CA

MacGregor, Jim
Guidance Director
Pike High School
Indianapolis, IN

Martin, Patricia
School Counselor Liaison
The College Board
Washington, DC

Meyers, Paul
Consultant
California Department of Education
Sacramento, CA

Myrick, Robert
Professor
University of Florida
Gainesville, FL

Paisley, Pam
Associate Professor
The University of Georgia
Athens, GA

Reynolds, Sue
Guidance and Counseling Specialist
Indiana Department of Education
Indianapolis, IN

Rich, Dave
Director, Student Support Services
Antelope Valley Union High School District
Lancaster, CA

Stone, Carolyn
Associate Professor
University of North Florida
Jacksonville, FL

Turba, Robert
Chairperson of Guidance Services
Stanton College Preparatory School
Jacksonville, FL

Whitfield, Edwin
Associate Director
Ohio Department of Education
Columbus, OH

APPENDIX B

The National Standards for School Counseling Programs: What Students Should Know and Be Able To Do (ASCA, 1997)

The national standards identify the attitudes, knowledge, and skills that students should acquire in a proactive and preventive manner through a broad range of experiences. The adoption and implementation of the national standards also has changed the way school counseling programs are designed and delivered across our country. The emphasis is on academic success for all students, not only those students who are motivated, supported, and ready to learn. The school counseling program based upon the national standards supports every student to achieve success in school and to develop into a contributing member of our society.

The nine national standards are based on the three widely accepted and interrelated areas of student development as described in the counseling literature and research: academic, career and personal/social development.

ACADEMIC DEVELOPMENT

The three standards for academic development guide school counselors as they implement school counseling program strategies and activities to support and maximize student learning. Academic development includes students acquiring attitudes, knowledge, and skills that contribute to effective learning in school and throughout their lifespan; employing strategies to achieve success in school; and understanding the relationship of academics to the world of work, and to life at home and in the community. The academic development standards are:

Standard A. Students will acquire the attitudes, knowledge, and skills that contribute to effective learning in school and throughout their life span.

Standard B. Students will complete school with the academic preparation essential to choose from a wide variety of substantial post-secondary options, including college.

Standard C. Students will understand the relationship of academics to the world of work, and to life at home, and in the community.

CAREER DEVELOPMENT

The standards for career development guide school counselors as they implement school counseling program strategies and activities to assist students acquire attitudes, knowledge, and skills to successfully transition from grade to grade, from school to post-secondary education, and ultimately to the world of work. Career development activities include the employment of strategies to achieve future career success and job satisfaction, as well as fostering understanding of the relationship between personal qualities, education and training, and future career goals. The three career development standards are:

Standard A. Students will acquire the skills to investigate the world of work in relation to knowledge of self and to make informed career decisions.

Standard B. Students will employ strategies to achieve future career success and satisfaction.

Standard C. Students will understand the relationship between personal qualities, education and training, and the world of work.

PERSONAL-SOCIAL DEVELOPMENT

The standards for personal-social development guide school counselors as they implement school counseling program strategies and activities to provide personal and social growth experiences to facilitate students' progress through school and make the transition to adulthood. Personal-social development contributes to academic and career success, and includes the acquisition of attitudes, knowledge, and skills to help students understand and respect self and others, acquire effective interpersonal skills, understand safety and survival skills, and develop into contributing members of society. The three personal-social development standards are:

Standard A. Students will acquire the attitudes, knowledge, and interpersonal skills to help them understand and respect self and others.

Standard B. Students will make decisions, set goals, and take appropriate action to achieve goals.

Standard C. Students will understand safety and survival skills.

Please note: The National Standards for School Counseling Programs are currently in revision with a tentative release date of Fall 2010. For further information, check the American School Counselor Association (ASCA) website http://www.schoolcounselor.org

Appendix C

American School Counselor Association National Model: A Framework For School Counseling Programs

The recently released ASCA National Model (ASCA, 2003, 2005) reinforces the importance of delivering a comprehensive, developmental, and results-based program that carefully considers local demographic needs and the political climate of the community. The four main components of the model are: 1) the foundation of the program requires the implementation of the belief and mission that every student will benefit form the school counseling program; 2) the delivery system defines the implementation process and the components of the comprehensive model, i.e., guidance curriculum, individual planning with students, responsive services, and system support; 3) the management system presents the organizational processes and tools needed to deliver a comprehensive school counseling program. These processes and tools include: agreements of responsibility, use of data, action plans for guidance curriculum and closing the gap, and time and task analysis; and, 4) the accountability system helps school counselors demonstrate the effectiveness of their work in measurable terms such as impact over time, performance evaluation, and a program audit.

The National Model speaks to the importance of having an organizational framework that documents and demonstrates "how are students different as a result of the school counseling program?" A commitment to accountability shifts public perception from questions such as "what do school counselors really do?" to showing how school counselors are key players in the academic success story for students and also partners in student achievement.

ASCA NATIONAL MODEL FOR SCHOOL COUNSELING PROGRAMS

The four main components of the model are: 1) the foundation of the program requires the implemen-

tation of the belief and mission that every student will benefit form the school counseling program; 2) the delivery system defines the implementation process and the components of the comprehensive model, i.e., guidance curriculum, individual planning with students, responsive services, and system support; 3) the management system presents the organizational processes and tools needed to deliver a comprehensive school counseling program. These processes and tools include: agreements of responsibility, use of data, action plans for guidance curriculum and closing the gap, and time and task analysis; and, 4) the accountability system helps school counselors demonstrate the effectiveness of their work in measurable terms such as impact over time, performance evaluation, and a program audit.

Appendix D

Critical Data Examples

Measures of Achievement:

Test Results

State Exams such as the Florida Comprehensive Achievement Test (FCAT); Texas Assessment of Knowledge and Skills (TAKS); New York State Regents Exams, etc.

Preliminary Scholastic Achievement Test (PSAT)

Scholastic Achievement Test (SAT)

ACT

ASVAB

Standardized achievement tests such as the CTBS, Iowa Tests, Stanford Achievement Tests, NAEP, etc.

Other Measures of Student Achievement

Ninth grade promotion rate

Retention rates

Drop-out Rates

Postsecondary enrollment

(four-year-college, community college, apprenticeship, career and technical, military training)

Grade Point Averages

Rank in Class Ninth grade promotion rate

Impacts on Achievement

Course enrollment patterns that demonstrate commitment to high achievement

Numbers of National Merit/Achievement Semi-Finalists

Enrollment In Honors, AP, IB, or College Level Courses

Enrollment In General, Remedial Courses.

Exceptional Student/Special Education Screening and Placement

Gifted Screening and Enrollment

Alternative School Enrollment

Demographics of the Internal and External School Community

Entry and Withdrawal Information

Ethnicity

Gender

Number and Type of Discipline Referrals to include Suspension Rate

Attendance Rate

Single Family Situations

School geographic areas

Free/Reduced Lunch Students and other available Socio-Economic Measures

History And Patterns of Changes in Community

Community Crime Rate

Remember, a quick look at data alone does not tell the whole story. It is important to disaggregate all critical data elements and look at them in terms of gender, race/ethnicity, socio-economic status, and perhaps by teacher to shed light on areas of success or areas in need of attention.

Other important data elements include:

- Course taking patterns in rigorous academic program.
- Course Pass/Fail Rates.
- Number of credits taken per year.
- Discipline/Suspension Rates.
- Gifted and Talented Program Enrollment.
- Graduation Rates.
- Definitive Exit Plans for 12th Graders.
- Honor Roll.
- Promotion/Retention rates.